BTEC Level 3 National Study Skills Guide in Sport

Welcome to your Study Skills Guide! You can make it your own – start by adding your personal and course details below...

Learner's name: _____

BTEC course title: _____

Date started: _____

Mandatory units:

_____

_____

_____

Optional units:

_____

_____

_____

Centre name: _____

Centre address:

_____

_____

_____

Tutor's name: _____

Published by Pearson Education Limited, a company incorporated in England and Wales, having its registered office at Edinburgh Gate, Harlow, Essex, CM20 2JE. Registered company number: 872828

Edexcel is a registered trademark of Edexcel Limited

Text © Pearson Education Limited 2010

First published 2010

18

20 19

British Library Cataloguing in Publication Data

A catalogue record for this book is available from the British Library

ISBN 978 1 84690 659 6

Typeset and edited by DSM Partnership
Cover design by Visual Philosophy, created by eMC Design
Cover photo/illustration © Getty Images: Greg Pease/Stone
Printed and bound by L.E.G.O. S.p.A. Lavis (TN) - Italy

Acknowledgements

The author and publisher would like to thank the following individuals and organisations for permission to reproduce photographs:

Alamy Images: Angela Hampton Picture Library 19, Claudia Wiens 66; Corbis: 76; iStockphoto: Gene Chutka 10, Barbara Sauder 7, Chris Schmidt 33; Pearson Education Ltd: Steve Shott 28, Ian Wedgewood.

All other images © Pearson Education.

Every effort has been made to contact copyright holders of material reproduced in this book. Any omissions will be rectified in subsequent printings if notice is given to the publishers.

Websites

Go to www.pearsonhotlinks.co.uk to gain access to the relevant website links and information on how they can aid your studies. When you access the site, search for either the title BTEC Level 3 National Study Skills Guide in Sport or the ISBN 978184606596.

Disclaimer

This material has been published on behalf of Edexcel and offers high-quality support for the delivery of Edexcel qualifications.

This does not mean that the material is essential to achieve any Edexcel qualification, nor does it mean that it is the only suitable material available to support any Edexcel qualification. Edexcel material will not be used verbatim in setting any Edexcel examination or assessment. Any resource lists produced by Edexcel shall include this and other appropriate resources.

Copies of official specifications for all Edexcel qualifications may be found on the Edexcel website: www.edexcel.com

Contents

Popular progression pathways

General qualification	Vocationally related qualification	Applied qualification
Undergraduate Degree	BTEC Higher National	Foundation Degree
GCE AS and A level	BTEC National	Advanced Diploma

Ten steps to success in your BTEC Level 3 National

This Study Skills Guide has been written to help you achieve the best result possible on your BTEC Level 3 National course. At the start of a new course you may feel quite excited but also a little apprehensive. Taking a BTEC Level 3 National qualification has many benefits and is a major stepping-stone towards your future career. Using this Study Skills Guide will help you get the most out of your course from the start.

TOP TIP

Use this Study Skills Guide at your own pace. Dip in to find what you need. Look back at it whenever you have a problem or query.

During **induction** sessions at the start of your course, your tutor will explain important information, but it can be difficult to remember everything, and that's when you'll find this Study Skills Guide invaluable. Look at it whenever you want to check anything related to your course. It provides all the essential facts you need and has a Useful terms section to explain specialist terms, words and phrases, including some that you will see highlighted in this book in bold type.

This Study Skills Guide covers the skills you'll need to do well in your course – such as managing your time, researching and analysing information and preparing a presentation.

- Use the **Top tips** to make your life easier as you go.
- Use the **Key points** to help you to stay focused on the essentials.
- Use the **Action points** to check what you need to know or do now.
- Use the **Case studies** to relate information to your chosen sector and vocational area.

- Use the **Activities** to test your knowledge and skills.
- Use the **Useful terms** section to check the meaning of specialist terms.

This Study Skills Guide has been designed to work alongside the Edexcel Student Book for BTEC Level 3 National Sport (Edexcel, 2010). This Student Book includes the main knowledge you'll need, with tips from BTEC experts, Edexcel assignment tips, assessment activities and up-to-date case studies from industry experts, plus handy references to your Study Skills Guide.

This Study Skills Guide is divided into ten steps, each relating to a key aspect of your studies, from understanding assessment to time management to maximising opportunities. Concentrate on getting things right one step at a time. Thousands of learners have achieved BTEC Level 3 National qualifications and are now studying for a degree or building a successful career at work. Using this Study Skills Guide, and believing in your own abilities, will help you achieve your future goals, too.

Introduction to the sport sector

Sport is a huge industry and is still continuing to grow. The London 2012 Olympic and Paralympic Games are giving a further boost to the sector, and it is anticipated that many people will be encouraged and inspired to take up sport as part of the drive to get the nation active.

The fitness industry is also a large and growing industry. In 2009 there were almost seven million people in the UK who were members of a gym or a leisure centre. This figure is predicted to increase as people realise that an active lifestyle is a healthier one.

You are starting on a BTEC Level 3 National in Sport or a BTEC Level 3 National in Sport and Exercise Sciences. These are two of the most popular BTEC courses currently available.

The BTEC Level 3 National in Sport and Exercise Sciences qualification will help to prepare you for a range of careers in sport and exercise sciences and for higher education in this field.

If you are taking the BTEC Level 3 National in Sport at Diploma or Extended Diploma level, there are three different pathways that you can follow. The pathway is usually selected before you start the course.

Each pathway covers different possible careers in the sport and leisure industry. These are designed to give you the knowledge and experience required to help you to either progress directly into your ideal job or allow you to advance to further training and/or qualifications in order to get the job of your dreams.

Pathways on BTEC Level 3 National Diplomas and National Extended Diplomas in Sport

There are three pathways at Diploma and Extended Diploma level:

- Performance and Excellence
- Development, Coaching and Fitness
- Outdoor Adventure

The **Performance and Excellence pathway** is designed for people who are thinking of pursuing, or are currently involved in, a career as an elite sports performer. The BTEC National in Sport (Performance and Excellence) will help you prepare for becoming an elite performer in a variety of ways. You will study several specialist units, which will be selected by your tutor. Each of these units is designed to help you gain a better understanding of how a performer's body, mind, diet, technical ability and tactical skills can have a huge impact on sports performance so that each factor can be assessed and reviewed to improve your own or another person's sporting performance.

Some of the units you might study on this pathway include:

- Unit 7: Fitness Testing for Sport and Exercise
- Unit 11: Sports Nutrition
- Unit 17: Psychology for Sports Performance
- Unit 12: Current Issues in Sport
- Unit 15: Instructing Physical Activity and Exercise
- Unit 18: Sports Injuries
- Unit 27: Technical and Tactical Skills in Sport
- Unit 28: The Athlete's Lifestyle
- Unit 39: Sports Facilities and Operational Management

The **Development, Coaching and Fitness pathway** is designed for someone who wants to progress into a career in sports development or sports coaching, or who wants to work in the fitness industry. Research demonstrates a clear link between an active lifestyle and good health. As a result, the health and fitness industry has grown substantially over the last 10 years, and it will probably continue to grow. This means that there is a demand for exercise professionals and there are good employment opportunities. Both sports coaches and sports development officers are required to meet the growing demand for participation in sport. They are also needed to help raise performance standards.

The BTEC Level 3 National in Sport (Development, Coaching and Fitness) will prepare you for these different careers in a variety of ways. You will study several specialist units, which will be selected by your tutor. Each of these units is designed to help you gain a better understanding of the sports industry. You will gain knowledge about sports and leisure facility operations, sports development, coaching techniques and training methods, and learn how to plan and lead an exercise session.

Some of the units you might study on this pathway include:

- Unit 5: Sports Coaching
- Unit 8: Practical Team Sports

The Development, Coaching and Fitness pathway may help you work towards a job in personal training.

- Unit 9: Practical Individual Sports
- Unit 13: Leadership in Sport
- Unit 14: Exercise, Health and Lifestyle
- Unit 21: Sport and Exercise Massage
- Unit 41: Profiling Sports Performance.

The **Outdoor Adventure pathway** is designed for people who are thinking about pursuing a career in the outdoor sector. This includes outdoor education, recreation and outdoor sport development. The outdoors sector has expanded significantly over the years, and it is continuing to grow. This means that there is a growing demand for outdoor education professionals, so there are good employment opportunities.

The BTEC Level 3 National in Sport (Outdoor Adventure) will prepare you for a career in the outdoor sector in a variety of ways, and the course includes taking part in a multi-day expedition, and in land-based and water-based outdoor and adventurous activities.

Some of the units you might study on this pathway include:

- Unit 13: Leadership in Sport
- Unit 29: Principles and Practices in Outdoor Adventure
- Unit 30: Equipment and Facilities for Outdoor and Adventurous Activities
- Unit 31: Impact and Sustainability in Outdoor Adventure
- Unit 32: Environmental Education for Outdoor Adventure
- Unit 33: Skills for Land-based Outdoor and Adventurous Activities
- Unit 34: Skills for Water-based Outdoor and Adventurous Activities
- Unit 37: Outdoor and Adventurous Expeditions
- Unit 38: Alternative Pursuits for Outdoor Adventure

Skills for the sport sector

There is a huge range of careers available in the sport and leisure industry, from leisure centre management, coaching, officiating and sports journalism to fitness instructing. Elite performers may even play sport at professional level.

For most careers in the sport and leisure industry you will need:

- good communication skills
- good interpersonal skills

- the ability to work well as a member of a team
- the ability to lead a team
- the ability to manage your time effectively.

Studying for a BTEC Level 3 National in Sport or Sport and Exercise Sciences allows you to practise these skills through the styles of teaching that you will encounter and the methods that are used to assess your understanding and knowledge of the different subject areas.

Step One: Understand your course and how it works

Case study: Making the right choice

Andy, Charlotte, Tyrone and Wahid are starting BTEC Level 3 National Diplomas in Sport or Sport and Exercise Sciences. All four learners are interested in sport and plan to pursue a career in the sports industry. However, each learner will be taking a different pathway so that they can follow their individual interests and pursue their potential career choices.

Andy is in a football youth academy and he hopes to become a professional footballer. He is going to take a BTEC Level 3 National Diploma in Sport (Performance and Excellence). The course will help him to understand how his body responds to exercise and how to get the best out of his training. It will also help him to develop the rigour and discipline needed by a professional footballer.

Charlotte has always loved taking part in outdoor pursuits, and she especially enjoys sailing and windsurfing. She hopes one day to work as an instructor in an outdoor pursuits centre. The course that she will be studying is the BTEC Level 3 National Diploma in Sport (Outdoor Adventure). She will take units about how her body works and responds to exercise, but she will also have the opportunity to take part in a range of outdoor pursuits as part of her course. This will help her improve her techniques and performance in each activity.

Tyrone plans to work in a gym and he also wants to become a personal trainer. He will be taking the BTEC Level 3 National Diploma in Sport (Development, Coaching and Fitness). Like the other two sport pathways, this examines the body and how it responds to exercise, but Tyrone will also have the chance to learn how to instruct exercise classes and devise training programmes. This will help him to fulfil his plans for his future career.

Wahid is taking the BTEC Level 3 National Diploma in Sport and Exercise Sciences. He hopes to become a sports scientist one day. He will learn about anatomy, how the body moves and how to carry out research. This will help Wahid gain the knowledge he needs to get accepted on a higher education course, which he will need to pursue his career aspirations.

Reflection point

In small groups, discuss what sort of career you would like in the sport and active leisure industry. Think about the areas that interest you, and the sort of experiences that you have had which make you think that this industry would suit you. Think about which qualification and pathway would best suit your career aspirations.

All BTEC Level 3 National qualifications are **vocational** or **work-related**. This means that you gain specific knowledge and understanding relevant to your chosen area. It gives you several advantages when you start work. For example, you will already know quite a lot about your chosen area, which will help you settle down more quickly. If you are already employed, you become more valuable to your employer.

Your BTEC course will prepare you for the work you want to do.

There are four types of BTEC Level 3 National qualification: Certificates, Subsidiary Diplomas, Diplomas and Extended Diplomas

	Certificate	Subsidiary Diploma	Diploma	Extended Diploma
Credit	30	60	120	180
Equivalence	1 AS level	1 A level	2 A levels	3 A levels

These qualifications are often described as **nested**. This means that they fit inside each other (rather like Russian dolls) because the same units are common to each qualification – so you can progress from one to another easily by completing more units.

TOP TIP

The structure of BTEC Level 3 National qualifications means it's easy to progress from one type to another and gain more credits, as well as to specialise in particular areas that interest you.

- Every BTEC Level 3 National qualification has a set number of **mandatory units** that all learners must complete.
- All BTEC Level 3 National qualifications include **optional units** that enable you to study particular areas in more depth.

- Some BTEC Level 3 National qualifications have **specialist pathways**, which may have additional mandatory units. These specialist pathways allow you to follow your career aims more precisely. For example, if you are studying to become an IT practitioner, you can choose pathways in software development, networking, systems support or IT and business.

- On all BTEC courses you are expected to be responsible for your own learning. Obviously your tutor will give you help and guidance when necessary, but you also need to be 'self-starting' and able to use your own initiative. Ideally, you can also assess how well you are doing and make improvements when necessary.

- BTEC Level 3 National grades convert to UCAS points, just like A-levels, but the way you are assessed and graded on a BTEC course is different, as you will see in the next section.

Key points

- You can study part-time or full-time for your BTEC Level 3 National.

- You can do a Certificate, Subsidiary Diploma, Diploma or Extended Diploma, and progress easily from one to the other.

- You will study both mandatory units and optional units on your course.

- When you have completed your BTEC course you can get a job (or **apprenticeship**), use your qualification to develop your career and/or continue studying to degree level.

- On all BTEC Level 3 National courses, the majority of your learning is practical and vocationally focused to develop the skills you need for your chosen career.

Using the Edexcel website to find out about your course

- You can check all the details about your BTEC Level 3 National course on the Edexcel website – go to www.edexcel.com.

- Enter the title of your BTEC Level 3 National qualification in the qualifications finder.

- Now find the specification in the list of documents. This is a long document so don't try to print it. Instead, look at the information on the units you will be studying to see the main topics you will cover.

- Then save the document or bookmark the page so that you can easily refer to it again if you need to.

Action points

1 By discussing with your tutor and by exploring the Edexcel website, find out the key information about your course and use it to complete the 'Important information' form on the next page. You can refer to this form at any time to refresh your memory about any part of your studies.

a) Check whether you are studying for a BTEC Level 3 Certificate, Subsidiary Diploma, Diploma or Extended Diploma, and find out the number of units you will be studying.

b) Find out the titles of the mandatory units you will be studying.

c) Find out the titles of the optional units and identify the ones offered at your centre.

d) Check the length of your course, and when you will be studying each unit.

e) Identify the optional units you will be taking. On some National courses you will do this at the start, while on others you may make your final decision later.

f) Find out other relevant information about your BTEC Level 3 National qualification. Your centre may have already given you details about the course structure.

g) Ask your tutor to help you to complete section 10 on the form. Depending on your course, you may be developing specific additional or personal skills – such as personal, learning and thinking skills (PLTS) and functional skills – or spending time on work experience, going on visits, or doing other activities linked to your subject area.

h) Talk to your tutor about section 12 on the form, as your sources of information will depend on the careers guidance and information at your centre. You may find it useful to exchange ideas with other members of your class.

	IMPORTANT INFORMATION ON MY BTEC LEVEL 3 NATIONAL COURSE
1	The title of the BTEC Level 3 National qualification I am studying is:
2	The length of my course is:
3	The total number of units I will study is:
4	The number of mandatory units I have to study is:
5	The titles of these mandatory units and the dates (or terms) when I will study them are:
6	The main topics I will learn in each mandatory unit include:

IMPORTANT INFORMATION ON MY BTEC LEVEL 3 NATIONAL COURSE	
7	The number of optional units I have to study is:
8	The titles of the optional units I will study are:
9	The main topics I will learn in each optional unit include:
10	Other important aspects of my course are:
11	After I have achieved my BTEC Level 3 National my options include:
12	Useful sources of information I can use to find out more about these options include:

2 Many learners already have information, contacts or direct experience that relate to their course. For example, you may have a specific interest or hobby that links to a unit, such as being a St John Ambulance cadet if you are studying Public Services. Think about the relevant sources of information you already have access to and complete the table below.

MY INFORMATION SOURCES	
Experts I know	(Who they are, what they know)
My hobbies and interests	(What they are, what they involve)
My job(s)	(Past and present work and work experience, and what I did)
Programmes I like to watch	(What these are, how they relate to my course)
Magazines and/or books I read	(What these are, examples of relevant articles)
ICT sources	(My centre's intranet as well as useful websites)
Other	(Other sources relevant for my particular course and the topics I will be studying)

Activity: Referencing your work

To find out further information and to produce evidence to support your assignment work, you will need to carry out research using textbooks, journals and websites. When presenting your work, you will need to know how to reference any sources that you cite, using the Harvard referencing system.

This activity helps you to learn how to use this system.

1 Go to your library and find books that include information about one of the subjects you are studying on your course.

2 Write the title of each book, plus the name(s) of the authors and information about the publisher in the table below.

Author(s) name(s)	Book title and edition	Publisher and publisher's location (remember to also list the page numbers where you found the information)

3 Summarise how you could use each book to support your assignment work.

You could use a table such as the one below for this.

Title of book	
What can this be used for?	
Title of book	
What can this be used for?	
Title of book	
What can this be used for?	

4 Show how you would list each book in the references for your written work. Use the Harvard referencing system. To do this, you will need to use this structure:

Author(s) surname and initials (Year), *Book title* and edition (if not the first), publisher: publisher location, page numbers (if appropriate).

For example:

Adams, M. et al. (2010) *BTEC Level 3 National Sport (Performance and Excellence) Student Book*, Pearson: Oxford

Adams, M. et al. (2010) *BTEC Level 3 National Sport (Development, Coaching and Fitness) Student Book*, Pearson: Oxford

If a book has more than two authors, it is the convention to list just one author followed by 'et al.'. The 'et al.' is short for a Latin phrase meaning 'and others'. The two books cited above both have seven authors, so only Adams, M. (Mark Adams) is listed. Either list the author who comes first alphabetically or the most important author. In this case, Mark Adams is not only the first name when the authors are listed in alphabetical order, but he is also the lead author for both books.

Step Two: Understand how you are assessed and graded

Case study: Assignments and grading – Andy's experience

Andy enjoys sports and physical exercise. He likes to think about issues and problems and come up with ideas while exercising. Andy communicates using extravagent hand gestures and other 'loud' body language. He can't sit still for long, he finds that he learns best when actively involved in learning. Andy appears to be a kinaesthetic learner.

Part of the reasoning behind Andy's decision to take a BTEC Level 3 National in Sport was that he liked the fact that tutors assessed learners through a range of methods, including practical demonstrations. For example, a tutor could observe a learner display skill in an activity such as tennis or football, and make comments on an observation checklist. Learners might also be assessed through delivering a presentation, designing a poster or promotional leaflet, completing a logbook or training diary, or taking part in an experiment and producing a lab report.

Andy is a learner who likes to be active, and he would much rather be assessed through doing some sort of practical activity. Many other learners also prefer types of assessment

that involve doing something other than taking lecture notes and producing essays.

Andy has found several ways to help him to get the most out of his studies. Wherever possible, he tries to touch objects as he learns about what they do. For example, in anatomy lessons, he handles the models of the skeleton and he moves the bones and the joints around to help him learn their postions and to visualise how they work in the body.

He uses cards to make notes about important information that he can use when creating and delivering presentations. He draws spider diagrams to help him to relate one piece of information to another, such as the various components of physical and skill-related fitness.

Reflection points

How do you learn best? Is it, like Andy, through active participation? How do you like to be assessed – by producing a report, doing a presentation or practically demonstrating your skills?

Your assessment

This section looks at the importance of your assignments, how they are graded, and how this converts into unit points and UCAS points. Unlike A-levels, there are no externally-set final exams on a BTEC course. Even if you know this because you already have a BTEC First qualification, you should still read this section, as now you will be working at a different level.

Your learning is assessed by **assignments**, set by your tutors. You will complete these throughout

your course, using many different **assessment methods**, such as real-life case studies, **projects** and presentations. Some assignments may be work-based or **time-constrained** – it depends very much on the vocational area you are studying.

Your assignments are based on **learning outcomes** set by Edexcel. These are listed for each unit in your course specification. You must achieve **all** the learning outcomes to pass each unit.

TOP TIP

Check the learning outcomes for each unit by referring to the course specification – go to www.edexcel.com.

Important skills to help you achieve your grades include:

- researching and analysing information (see page 63)

- using your time effectively (see page 25)

- working co-operatively as a member of a team (see page 57.)

Your grades, unit points and UCAS points

On a BTEC Level 3 National course, assessments that meet the learning outcomes are graded as pass, merit or distinction. The different grades within each unit are set out by Edexcel as **grading criteria** in a **grading grid**. These criteria identify the **higher-level skills** you must demonstrate to achieve a higher grade (see also Step Six: Understand your assessment, on page 35).

All your assessment grades earn **unit points**. The total points you get for all your units determines your final qualification grade(s) – pass, merit or distinction. You get:

- one final grade if you are taking a Certificate or Subsidiary Diploma

- two final grades if you are taking a Diploma

- three final grades if you are taking an Extended Diploma.

Your points and overall grade(s) convert to **UCAS points**, which you need to be accepted onto a degree course. For example, if you achieve three final pass grades for your BTEC Level 3 Extended Diploma, you get 120 UCAS Tariff points. If you achieve three final distinction grades, this increases to 360 – equivalent to three GCE A-levels.

Please note that all UCAS information was correct at the time of going to print, but we would advise that you check the UCAS website for the most up to date information. See page 98 for how to access their website.

Case study: Securing a university place

Chris and Shaheeda both want a university place and have worked hard on their BTEC Level 3 Extended Diploma course.

Chris's final score is 226 unit points, which converts to 280 UCAS Tariff points. Shaheeda has a total score of 228 unit points – just two points more – which converts to 320 UCAS points! This is because a score of between 204 and 227 unit points gives 280 UCAS points, whereas a score of 228 to 251 points gives 320 UCAS points.

Shaheeda is delighted because this increases her chances of getting a place on the degree course she wants. Chris is annoyed. He says if he had realised, he would have worked harder on his last assignment to get two more points.

You start to earn points from your first assessment, so you get many benefits from settling in quickly and doing good work from the start. Understanding how **grade boundaries** work also helps you to focus your efforts to get the best possible final grade.

You will be able to discuss your learning experiences, your personal progress and the achievement of your learning objectives in **individual tutorials** with your tutor. These enable you to monitor your progress and overcome temporary difficulties. You can also talk about any worries you have. Your tutor is one of your most important resources, and a tutorial gives you their undivided attention.

You can talk through any questions or problems in your tutorials.

Key points

- Your learning is assessed in a variety of ways, such as by assignments, projects and real-life case studies.

- You need to demonstrate specific knowledge and skills to achieve the learning outcomes set by Edexcel. You must achieve all the grading criteria to pass a unit.

- The grading criteria for pass, merit and distinction are shown in a grading grid for the unit. Higher-level skills are needed for higher grades.

- The assessment grades of pass, merit and distinction convert to unit points. The total unit points you receive for the course determine your final overall grade(s) and UCAS points.

TOP TIP

It's always tempting to spend longer on work you like doing and are good at, but focusing on improving your weak areas will do more to boost your overall grade(s).

Action points

1 Find out more about your own course by carrying out this activity.

   a) Find the learning outcomes for the units you are currently studying. Your tutor may have given you these, or you can find them in your course specification – go to www.edexcel.com.

   b) Look at the grading grid for the units and identify the way the requirements change for the higher grades. If there are some unfamiliar words, check these in Step Six of this guide (see page 35 onwards).

   c) If the unit points system still seems complicated, ask your tutor to explain it.

   d) Check the UCAS points you would need for the course or university which interests you.

   e) Design a form you can use to record the unit points you earn throughout your course. Keep this up to date. Regularly check how your points relate to your overall grade(s), based on the grade boundaries for your qualification. Your tutor can give you this information, or you can check it yourself in the course specification.

Activity: Understanding how you are assessed and graded

To see how well you have grasped the main issues concerning assessment and grading, try to answer these questions about BTEC Nationals in Sport or Sport Exercise Sciences qualifications.

How many different types of assessment methods can you think of?

What are the four learning outcomes for Unit 7 Fitness Testing for Sport and Exercise (Sport) and Unit 8 Fitness Testing for Sport and Exercise (Sport and Exercise Sciences)?

Why do you think it is important to fully understand how your course is structured, how you are assessed and graded, and what are the possible progression routes?

Having read through this section dealing with how you are assessed and graded, list any areas or aspects that you are not quite clear about. Make a point of discussing these with your tutor to resolve any outstanding issues.

Step Three: Understand yourself

Case study: Being self-aware

Wahid studied GCSEs at school. He found that he did not perform particularly well under exam conditions. He got so nervous that he forgot much of what he had revised. However, he is very good at carrying out research and finding out about subjects that interest him. He works well as a member of a team, and Wahid feels that he is fair and open in discussions. Over the last few years, he has learnt how he 'ticks', which has helped him to decide the type of qualifications that would be the better choice for his studies at college.

'GCSEs were OK, but most of the coursework involved writing long essays. This took ages and was quite boring. We then had to sit in the school hall at the end of year 11 to take our GCSE exams. I get really nervous about exams, and I am sure I didn't do as well as I could have because my nerves made it difficult to concentrate. I did try different forms of relaxation before an exam and I always spent plenty of time revising, but I never seemed to get the results my teachers thought that I was capable of achieving.

'I was really pleased to find out from the tutor who interviewed me that we won't have any formal exams on the BTEC Level 3 National in Sport and Exercise Sciences. All assessment will be on coursework. Even better is the fact that the coursework won't consist of doing long essays.

'I was also told that some of our assessments will be through observation. We actually get to do an activity and the tutor observes us doing it – so I'm looking forward to demonstrating my football skills as part of one of my assessments in the future. We are also going to be assessed through presentations and other 'hands-on' activities. I prefer this kind of assessment – I can be creative and apply my knowledge, rather than just writing out loads of information.'

Reflection points

Why do you think Wahid's personality makes him suited to the BTEC way of learning? What aspects of your personality will help you on your course?

Self-awareness means understanding how you 'tick'. For example, do you prefer practical activities rather than theory? Do you prefer to draw or sketch an idea, rather than write about it?

Self-awareness is important as it makes you less reliant on other people's opinions and gives you confidence in your own judgement. You can also reflect on your actions to learn from your experiences.

Self-awareness also means knowing your own strengths and weaknesses. Knowing your strengths enables you to feel positive and confident about yourself and your abilities. Knowing your weaknesses means you know the areas you need to develop.

You can analyse yourself by looking at...

... your personality and preferences

You may have taken a personality test at your centre. If not, your tutor may recommend one to use, or there are many available online.

Many employers ask job candidates to complete a personality test so that they can match the type of work they are offering to the most suitable people. Although these tests can only give a broad indication of someone's personality they may help to avoid mismatches, such as hiring someone who is introverted to work in sales.

... your skills and abilities

To succeed in your assignments, and to progress in a career, requires a number of skills. Some may be vocationally-specific, or professional, skills that you can improve during your course – such as sporting performance on a Sports course. Others are broader skills that are invaluable no matter what you are studying – such as communicating clearly and co-operating with others.

You will work faster and more accurately, and have greater confidence, if you are skilled and proficient. A quick skills check will identify any problem areas.

TOP TIP

Use the Skills building section on page 87 to identify the skills you need for your course. You'll also find hints and tips for improving any weak areas.

Key points

- You need certain skills and abilities to get the most out of your BTEC Level 3 National course and to develop your career potential.
- Knowing your strengths and weaknesses is a sign of maturity. It gives you greater confidence in your abilities and enables you to focus on areas for improvement.

TOP TIP

You will find more help in this guide on developing your skills in using time wisely (Step Four), working as a member of a group (Step Seven), researching and analysing information (Step Eight) and making effective presentations (Step Nine).

Action points

1 Gain insight into your own personality by ticking **True** or **False** against each of the following statements. Be honest!

		True	False
a)	If someone annoys me, I can tell them about it without causing offence.		
b)	If someone is talking, I often interrupt them to give them my opinion.		
c)	I get really stressed if I'm under pressure.		
d)	I can sometimes become very emotional and upset on other people's behalf.		
e)	I sometimes worry that I can't cope and may make a mess of something.		
f)	I am usually keen, enthusiastic and motivated to do well.		
g)	I enjoy planning and organising my work.		
h)	I find it easy to work and co-operate with other people and take account of their opinions.		
i)	I am easily influenced by other people.		
j)	I often jump to conclusions and judge people and situations on first impressions.		
k)	I prefer to rely on facts and experience rather than following my instincts.		

Now identify which of the skills and qualities in the box below will be really important in your chosen career.

> tact   truthfulness   listening skills
>
> **staying calm under pressure**
>
> **empathy with others**   self-confidence
>
> **initiative**   **planning and organising**
>
> **working with others**   self-assurance
>
> **objective judgements**

Use your answers to identify areas you should work on to be successful in the future.

2 As part of the UCAS process, all **higher education** applicants have to write a personal statement. This is different from a CV, which is a summary of achievements that all job applicants prepare. You may have already prepared a CV but not thought about a personal statement. Now is your chance!

Read the information about personal statement in the box. Then answer these questions:

a) Explain why personal statements are so important for higher education applicants.

b) Why do you think it is important for your personal statement to read well and be error-free?

c) Suggest three reasons why you shouldn't copy a pre-written statement you have found online.

d) Look at some websites to see what to include in the statement and how to set it out.

e) Prepare a bullet point list of ten personal facts. Focus on your strengths and good reasons why you should be given a place on the higher education course of your choice. If possible, discuss your list with your tutor. Then keep it safe, as it will be useful if you need to write a personal statement later.

Personal statements

This is the information that all higher education applicants have to put in the blank space on their UCAS form. The aim is to sell yourself to admissions tutors. It can be pretty scary, especially if you haven't written anything like it before.

So, where do you start?

First, **never** copy pre-written statements you find online. These are just for guidance. Even worse are websites that offer to write your statement for a fee, and send you a few general, pre-written paragraphs. Forget them all: you can do better!

Imagine you are an admissions tutor with 60 places to offer to 200 applicants. What will you need to read in a personal statement to persuade you to offer the applicant a place?

Most likely, clear explanations about:

- what the applicant can contribute to the course
- why the applicant really wants a place on your course
- what the applicant has done to further his/her own interests in this area, such as voluntary work
- attributes that show this applicant would be a definite bonus – such as innovative ideas, with evidence eg 'I organised a newsletter which we published every three months …'

A personal statement should be well written, with no grammatical or spelling errors, and organised into clear paragraphs.

For further guidance on personal statements, go to page 98 to find out how to access a number of helpful websites.

Activity: Writing your personal statement

It is a good idea to start thinking about what you plan to write in your personal statement. The information in your personal statement will not only be useful for helping you secure a place at university, but it may also be useful when writing a covering letter for a part-time job or work experience.

What courses are you interested in?

What experience have you had that relates to these courses? If you have not had any, how could you get some relevant experience?

What relevant qualifications do you have for these courses? If you have none, what qualifications would be helpful, and how and where could you get them?

How do you spend your free time ? Do you have any hobbies?

What other skills and qualities do you possess?

Step Four: Use your time wisely

Case study: Juggling demands on your time

Samantha is 18 years old and is studying for a BTEC Level 3 National in Sport and Exercise Sciences qualification. She has a part-time job working as a lifeguard at a leisure centre. She uses the money to help to pay for her car, which she uses to get to and from school, and to meet her study expenses, such as paying for textbooks and school trips.

She usually works two evenings a week and one day at the weekend, and most of the time this does not interfere with her school work. However, there are times when Samantha has to go in to work at short notice to cover shifts for people when they are ill. This can mean that Samantha does not have enough time to finish her coursework properly. She either misses the hand-in date or hands in work that is below her usual standard.

Samantha needs to learn to meet the demands of her course. She wants to attain the best grades that she is capable of, yet still juggle the demands of her job. She talks with her tutors and they decide that the best course of action is for Samantha to design a coursework diary. She should also start working on any coursework as soon as it is handed out so that assignments are completed before the due date. She must also learn to say 'no' to extra work shifts at the leisure centre if she knows from checking her coursework diary that she has a lot of work to complete.

Reflection point

What commitments do you have outside of school or college? How do you think you could best manage the demands of coursework and your outside commitments?

Most learners have to combine course commitments with other responsibilities such as a job (either full-time or part-time) and family responsibilities. You will also want to see your friends and keep up your hobbies and interests. Juggling these successfully means you need to be able to use your time wisely.

This involves planning what to do and when to do it to prevent panics about unexpected deadlines. As your course progresses, this becomes even more important as your workload may increase towards the end of a term. In some cases, there could be two or more assignments to complete simultaneously. Although tutors try to avoid clashes of this sort, it is sometimes inevitable.

To cope successfully, you need time-management skills, in particular:

- how to organise your time to be more productive
- how to prioritise tasks
- how to overcome time-wasters.

Organising your time

- **Use a diary or wall chart.**
  Using a different colour pen for each, enter:
  - your course commitments, such as assignment dates, tutorials, visits
  - important personal commitments, such as sports matches, family birthdays
  - your work commitments.

  TOP TIP

  A diary is useful because you can update it as you go, but a wall chart gives you a better overview of your commitments over several weeks. Keep your diary or chart up to date, and check ahead regularly so that you have prior warning of important dates.

- **Identify how you currently use your time.**
  - Work out how much time you spend at your centre, at work, at home and on social activities.
  - Identify which commitments are vital and which are optional, so you can find extra time if necessary.
- **Plan and schedule future commitments.**
  - Write down any appointments and tasks you must do.
  - Enter assignment review dates and final deadline dates in different colours.
  - This should stop you from arranging a dental appointment on the same morning that you are due to give an important presentation – or planning a hectic social life when you have lots of course work to do.

- **Decide your best times for doing course work.**
  - Expect to do most of your course work in your own time.
  - Work at the time of day when you feel at your best.
  - Work regularly, and in relatively short bursts, rather than once or twice a week for very long stretches.
  - If you're a night owl, allow an hour to 'switch off' before you go to bed.
- **Decide where to work.**
  - Choose somewhere you can concentrate without interruption.
  - Make sure there is space for resources you use, such as books or specialist equipment.
  - You also need good lighting and a good – but not too comfortable – chair.
  - If you can't find suitable space at home, check out your local or college library.
- **Assemble the items you need.**
  - Book ahead to get specific books, journals or DVDs from the library.
  - Ensure you have your notes, handouts and assignment brief with you.
  - Use sticky notes to mark important pages in textbooks or folders.

  TOP TIP

  Set yourself a target when you start work, so that you feel positive and productive at the end. Always try to end a session when a task is going well, rather than when you are stuck. Then you will be keener to go back to it the next day. Note down outstanding tasks you need to continue with next time.

- **Plan ahead.**
  - If anything is unclear about an assignment, ask your tutor for an explanation as soon as you can.
  - Break down assignments into manageable chunks, such as find information, decide what to use, create a plan for finished work, write rough draft of first section etc.
  - Work back from deadline dates so that you allow plenty of time to do the work.
  - Always allow more time than you need. It is better to finish early than to run out of time.

TOP TIP

If you are working on a task as a group, organise and agree times to work together. Make sure you have somewhere to meet where you can work without disturbing other courses or groups.

- **Be self-disciplined.**
  - Don't put things off because you're not in the mood. Make it easier by doing simple tasks first to get a sense of achievement. Then move on to something harder.
  - Plan regular breaks. If you're working hard, you need a change of activity to recharge your batteries.
  - If you have a serious problem or personal crisis, talk to your personal tutor promptly.

TOP TIP

Make sure you know the consequences of missing an assignment deadline, as well as the dispensations and exemptions that can be given if you have an unavoidable and serious problem, such as illness (see also page 36).

How to prioritise tasks

Prioritising means doing the most important and urgent task first. Normally this will be the task or assignment with the closest deadline or the one that will most affect your overall course grades.

One way of prioritising is to group tasks into ABC categories.

Category A tasks	These must be done now as they are very important and cannot be delayed, such as completing an assignment to be handed in tomorrow.
Category B tasks	These are jobs you should do if you have time, because otherwise they will rapidly become Category A, such as getting a book that you need for your next assignment.
Category C tasks	These are tasks you should do if you have the time, such as rewriting notes jotted down quickly in a lesson.

Expect to be flexible. For example, if you need to allow time for information to arrive, then send for this first. If you are working in a team, take into account other people's schedules when you are making arrangements.

Avoiding time-wasters

Everyone has days when they don't know where the time has gone. It may be because they were constantly interrupted or because things just kept going wrong. Whatever the reason, the end result is that some jobs don't get done.

If this happens to you regularly, you need to take steps to keep on track. Here are some useful tips.

- **Warn people in advance when you will be working.**
  - Ask them to not interrupt you.
  - If you are in a separate room, shut the door. If someone comes in, make it clear you don't want to talk.
  - If that doesn't work, find somewhere else (or some other time) to work.
- **Switch off your mobile, the television and radio, and your iPod/MP3 player.**
  - Don't respond to, or make, calls or texts.
  - If someone rings your home phone, let voicemail answer or ask them to call back later.
- **Be strict with yourself when you are working online.**
  - Don't check your email until you've finished work.
  - Don't get distracted when searching for information.
  - Keep away from social networking sites.
- **Avoid displacement activities.**
  - These are the normally tedious jobs, such as cleaning your computer screen, that suddenly seem far more attractive than working!

Talking to friends can occupy a lot of time.

TOP TIP

The first step in managing your own time is learning to say 'no' (nicely!) if someone asks you to do something tempting when you should be working.

Key points

- Being in control of your time allows you to balance your commitments according to their importance and means you won't let anyone down.
- Organising yourself and your time involves knowing how you spend your time now, planning when and where it is best to work, scheduling commitments and setting sensible timescales to complete your work.
- Knowing how to prioritise means you will schedule work effectively according to its urgency and importance. You will need self-discipline to follow the schedule you have set for yourself.
- Identifying ways in which you may waste time means you can guard against these to achieve your goals more easily.

TOP TIP

Benefits to managing your own time include being less stressed (because you are not reacting to problems or crises), producing better work and having time for a social life.

Action points

1 Start planning your time properly.

a) Find out how many assignments you will have this term, and when you will get them. Put this information into your diary or planner.

b) Update this with your other commitments for the term – both work-/course-related and social. Identify possible clashes and decide how to resolve the problem.

c) Identify one major task or assignment you will do soon. Divide it into manageable chunks and decide how long to allow for each chunk, plus some spare time for any problems. If possible, check your ideas with your tutor before you put them into your planner.

2 How good are you at being responsible for your own learning?

a) Fill in this table. Score yourself out of 5 for each area, where 0 is awful and 5 is excellent. Ask a friend or relative to score you as well. See if you can explain any differences.

	Scoring yourself	Other person's score for you
Being punctual		
Organisational ability		
Tidiness		
Working accurately		
Finding and correcting own mistakes		
Solving problems		
Accepting responsibility		
Working with details		
Planning how to do a job		
Using own initiative		
Thinking up new ideas		
Meeting deadlines		

b) Draw up your own action plan for areas where you need to improve. If possible, talk this through at your next **tutorial** (see page 18).

TOP TIP

Don't waste time doing things that distract you when studying for this course. In a sports business, time costs money.

Activity: Planning your time

As someone taking a BTEC Level 3 National in Sport or Sport and Exercise Sciences you probably spend some time taking part in sport as well as having other hobbies and pastimes that you enjoy in your spare time.

It can be difficult to fit in your usual activities when you have coursework to complete. A good way of working out your coursework time is to compile a weekly chart of your planned activities, then set aside some time every day or every other day for coursework. This will ensure that you are having time doing the things that you want to do and also have time for coursework.

Complete the weekly planner below, identifying 'free' time for you to do your coursework.

Day	Morning	Afternoon	Evening
Monday			
Tuesday			
Wednesday			
Thursday			
Friday			
Saturday			
Sunday			

Step Five: Utilise all your resources

Case study: Amy's successful assignment

Amy is taking a BTEC Level 3 National in Sport (Performance and Excellence). She always uses the course textbook to help her with her assignment research. However, one day, her college has a guest speaker delivering a presentation to her class. The speaker had been a hockey player for the Great Britain team, and she talked to the group about the lifestyle of an elite sports performer. Amy is a keen hockey player and hopes to one day play for her country, too.

At the end of the presentation, Amy asks several questions and receives some very interesting and informative answers. These answers really help Amy to understand one of the assignment tasks that she has been given. Amy uses these answers in her assignment, and she quotes the hockey player as the source of the information. For this assignment, Amy receives the highest grade that she has been awarded to date!

Textbooks, the internet and journals are all good methods of finding out information – but so are other people!

If you do not get the opportunity to listen to guest speakers in your school or college, you can try going to internet sites that have forums for learners to 'talk' to each other to get help. You may also find that a member of your family or a friend of the family has worked or competed in a sport that is relevant to your study. This person may be happy to talk about the experience.

Don't forget, you can always talk to your tutor too.

Reflection point

Do you know someone who works in the sport and leisure sector who may be able to help with your research into the industry?

Your resources are all the things that can help you to be successful in your BTEC Level 3 National qualification, from your favourite website to your **study buddy** (see page 32) who collects handouts for you if you miss a class.

Your centre will provide essential resources, such as a library with appropriate books and electronic reference sources, the computer network and internet access. You will have to provide basic resources such as pens, pencils and file folders yourself. If you have to buy your own textbooks, look after them carefully so you can sell them on at the end of your course.

Here is a list of resources, with tips for getting the best out of them.

- **Course information**. This includes your course specification, this Study Skills Guide and all information on the Edexcel website relating to your BTEC Level 3 National course. Course information from your centre will include term dates, assignment dates and your timetable. Keep everything safely so you can refer to it whenever you need to clarify something.
- **Course materials**. These include course handouts, printouts and your own notes and textbooks. Put handouts into an A4 folder as soon as you get them. Use a separate folder for each unit you study.

TOP TIP

Filing notes and handouts promptly means they don't get lost and will stay clean and uncrumpled, and you won't waste time looking for them.

- **Stationery**. You need pens and pencils, a notepad, a hole puncher, a stapler and sets of dividers. Dividers should be clearly labelled to help you store and quickly find notes, printouts and handouts. Your notes should be headed and dated, and those from your own research must also include your source (see Step Eight, page 57 onwards.)
- **People**. Your tutors, specialist staff at college, classmates, your employer and work colleagues, and your relatives and friends are all valuable resources. Many will have particular skills or work in the vocational area that you are studying. Talking to other learners can help to clarify issues that there may not have been time to discuss fully in class.

A **study buddy** is another useful resource as they can make notes and collect handouts if you miss a session. (Remember to return the favour when they are away.)

Always be polite when you are asking people for information. Prepare the questions first and remember that you are asking for help, not trying to get them to do the work for you! If you are interviewing someone for an assignment or project, good preparations are vital. (See Step Eight, page 57 onwards.)

If someone who did the course before you offers help, be careful. It is likely the course requirements will have changed. Never be tempted to copy their assignments (or someone else's). This is **plagiarism** – a deadly sin in the educational world (see also Step Six, page 35.)

TOP TIP

A positive attitude, an enquiring mind and the ability to focus on what is important will have a major impact on your final result.

Key points

- Resources help you to achieve your qualification. Find out what resources you have available to you and use them wisely.
- Have your own stationery items.
- Know how to use central facilities and resources such as the library, learning resource centres and your computer network. Always keep to the policy on IT use in your centre.
- People are a key resource – school or college staff, work colleagues, members of your class, friends, family and people who are experts in their field.

Action points

1 a) List the resources you will need to complete your course successfully. Identify which ones will be provided by your school or college, and which you need to supply yourself.

b) Go through your list again and identify the resources you already have (or know how to access) and those you don't.

c) Compare your list with a friend's and decide how to obtain and access the resources you need. Add any items to your list that you forgot.

d) List the items you still need to get and set a target date for doing this.

2 'Study buddy' schemes operate in many centres. Find out if this applies to your own centre and how you can make the best use of it.

In some you can choose your study buddy, in others people are paired up by their tutor.

- Being a study buddy might mean just collecting handouts when the other person is absent, and giving them important news.

- It may also mean studying together and meeting (or keeping in contact by phone or email) to exchange ideas and share resources.

With a study buddy you can share resources and stay on top of the course if you're ever away.

Activity: Resources

You will use many different resources while studying for a BTEC Level 3 National in Sport or Sport and Exercise Sciences – these will include textbooks, journals, CD-ROMs and internet sites.

Go to your school or college library and visit the sections that have material related to your qualification, such as information on sport, anatomy, physiology and sport psychology.

Spend some time on the internet looking at the types of resources available, then make a note of useful websites, writing a brief description of what each contains. This will help you when you begin to do assignments, as you will know which websites you can use as a starting point for your research.

Website address	Description of content

Now have a look at the available sport-related journals. Focus on a particular unit on your programme of study, and summarise articles that would be particularly useful as background reading or as sources of evidence that can be applied in your work.

Journal name	Description of content

Step Six: Understand your assessment

Case study: Asking for extra time on an assignment

Tyrone is taking a BTEC Level 3 National in Sport (Development, Coaching, and Fitness). He is enjoying the course and is just about managing to keep on track with his assignments.

'Doing the coursework does take up quite a bit of time. In the first term, when we got an assignment handed out to us, I used to always put it to one side and forget about it. I'd go to my usual five-a-side football games and do martial arts training three times a week, and I would watch sport on television in any free time. I'd then realise that I had work to be handed in and would madly rush to try to get it finished before it was due in. This meant that if I got stuck, I didn't have a chance to talk through any problems with my tutor, and I didn't get the grades I should have been able to achieve.

'Luckily we got the assignments back to see if we could improve our submissions after talking to our tutors, spending longer doing the research and taking more time on the final work. I am aiming to get distinctions for all my units, which means that I have to meet all the

pass, all the merit and all the distinction criteria for each unit. To help me do this, I now make sure that I make a start on each assignment as soon as possible. I often stay behind after a lesson to talk through anything that I don't understand about an assignment with my tutor before I get cracking on the research.

'As I am doing pretty well at my martial arts, I have now starting competing for my club. I make sure that this doesn't get in the way of my work. When I was asked to go to Holland for a week to compete for my club, which would have meant I would not get an assignment in on time, I spoke to my tutor about the opportunity to compete abroad and I was given an extension. I was also able to use some of the evidence I gathered during the competition to help meet the assessment requirements for a couple of units, which was great!'

Reflection points

How will you approach juggling your coursework and other commitments?

Being successful on any BTEC Level 3 National course means first understanding what you must do in your assignments – and then doing it.

Your assignments focus on topics you have already covered in class. If you've attended regularly, you should be able to complete them confidently.

However, there are some common pitfalls it's worth thinking about. Here are tips to avoid them:

- Read the instructions (the assignment brief) properly and several times before you start.
- Make sure you understand what you are supposed to do. Ask if anything is unclear.

- Complete every part of a task. If you ignore a question, you can't meet the grading criteria.
- Prepare properly. Do your research or reading before you start. Don't guess the answers.
- Communicate your ideas clearly. You can check this by asking someone who doesn't know the subject to look at your work.
- Only include relevant information. Padding out answers makes it look as if you don't know your subject.
- Do the work earlier rather than later to avoid any last-minute panics.
- Pay attention to advice and feedback that your tutor has given you.

The assignment 'brief'

This may be longer than its name implies! The assignment brief includes all the instructions for an assignment and several other details, as you can see in the table below.

What will you find in a BTEC Level 3 National assignment brief?	
Content	**Details**
Title	This will link to the unit and learning outcomes
Format/style	Written assignment, presentation, demonstration etc
Preparation	Read case study, do research etc
Learning outcomes	These state the knowledge you must demonstrate to obtain a required grade
Grading criterion/ criteria covered	For example, P1, M1, D1
Individual/group work	Remember to identify your own contribution in any group work
Feedback	Tutor, peer review
Interim review dates	Dates to see your tutor
Final deadline	Last submission date

Your centre's rules and regulations

Your centre will have several policies and guidelines about assignments, which you need to check carefully. Many, such as those listed below, relate to Edexcel policies and guidelines.

- The procedure to follow if you have a serious problem and can't meet a deadline. An extension may be granted.
- The penalty for missing a deadline without good reason.
- The penalty for copying someone else's work. This is usually severe, so never share your work (or CDs or USB flash drive) with anyone else, and don't borrow theirs.
- **Plagiarism** is also serious misconduct. This means copying someone's work or quoting from books and websites and pretending it is your own work.
- The procedure to follow if you disagree with the grade you are given.

Understanding the question or task

There are two aspects to a question or task. The first is the **command words**, which are described below. The second is the **presentation instructions**, which is what you are asked to do – don't write a report when you should be producing a chart!

Command words, such as 'explain', 'describe', 'analyse', 'evaluate' state how a question must be answered. You may be asked to 'describe' something at pass level, but you will need to do more, perhaps 'analyse' or 'evaluate', to achieve merit or distinction.

Many learners fail to achieve higher grades because they don't realise the difference between these words. Instead of analysing or evaluating they give an explanation instead. Adding more details won't achieve a higher grade – you need to change your whole approach to the answer.

The **grading grid** for each unit of your course gives you the command words, so that you know what to do to achieve a pass, merit or distinction. The tables that follow show you what is usually required when you see a particular command word. These are just examples to guide you, as the exact response will depend on the question. If you have any doubts, check with your tutor before you start work.

There are two important points to note.

- A command word such as 'create' or 'explain' may be repeated in the grading criteria for different grades. In these cases the complexity or range of the task itself increases at the higher grades.
- Command words vary depending on your vocational area. So Art and Design grading

grids may use different command words from Applied Science, for example.

To obtain a pass grade

To achieve a pass you must usually demonstrate that you understand the important facts relating to a topic and can state these clearly and concisely.

Command words for a pass	Meaning
Create (or produce)	Make, invent or construct an item.
Describe	Give a clear, straightforward description that includes all the main points and links these together logically.
Define	Clearly explain what a particular term means and give an example, if appropriate, to show what you mean.
Explain … how/why	Set out in detail the meaning of something, with reasons. It is often helpful to give an example of what you mean. Start with the topic then give the 'how' or 'why'.
Identify	Distinguish and state the main features or basic facts relating to a topic.
Interpret	Define or explain the meaning of something.
Illustrate	Give examples to show what you mean.
List	Provide the information required in a list rather than in continuous writing.
Outline	Write a clear description that includes all the main points but avoid going into too much detail.
Plan (or devise)	Work out and explain how you would carry out a task or activity.
Select (and present) information	Identify relevant information to support the argument you are making and communicate this in an appropriate way.
State	Write a clear and full account.
Undertake	Carry out a specific activity.
Examples:	
Identify the main features on a digital camera.	
Outline the steps to take to carry out research for an assignment.	

To obtain a merit grade

To obtain a merit you must prove that you can apply your knowledge in a specific way.

Command words for a merit	Meaning
Analyse	Identify separate factors and say how they relate to each other and how each one relates to the topic.
Classify	Sort your information into appropriate categories before presenting or explaining it.
Compare and contrast	Identify the main factors that apply in two or more situations and explain the similarities and differences or advantages and disadvantages.
Demonstrate	Provide several relevant examples or appropriate evidence which support the arguments you are making. In some vocational areas this may also mean giving a practical performance.
Discuss	Provide a thoughtful and logical argument to support the case you are making.
Explain (in detail)	Provide details and give reasons and/or evidence to clearly support the argument you are making.
Implement	Put into practice or operation. You may also have to interpret or justify the effect or result.
Interpret	Understand and explain an effect or result.
Justify	Give appropriate reasons to support your opinion or views and show how you arrived at these conclusions.
Relate/report	Give a full account, with reasons.
Research	Carry out a full investigation.
Specify	Provide full details and descriptions of selected items or activities.
Examples: Compare and contrast the performance of two different digital cameras. Explain in detail the steps to take to research an assignment.	

To obtain a distinction grade

To obtain a distinction you must prove that you can make a reasoned judgement based on appropriate evidence.

Command words for a distinction	Meaning
Analyse	Identify the key factors, show how they are linked, and explain the importance and relevance of each.
Assess	Give careful consideration to all the factors or events that apply, and identify which are the most important and relevant, with reasons.
Comprehensively explain	Give a very detailed explanation that covers all the relevant points, and give reasons for your views or actions.
Critically comment	Give your view after you have considered all the evidence, particularly the importance of both the relevant positive and negative aspects.
Evaluate	Review the information and then bring it together to form a conclusion. Give evidence to support each of your views or statements.
Evaluate critically	Review the information to decide the degree to which something is true, important or valuable. Then assess possible alternatives, taking into account their strengths and weaknesses if they were applied instead. Then give a precise and detailed account to explain your opinion.
Summarise	Identify/review the main relevant factors and/or arguments so that these are explained in a clear and concise manner.
Examples:	
Assess ten features commonly found on a digital camera.	
Analyse your own ability to carry out effective research for an assignment.	

TOP TIP

Check that you understand exactly how you need to demonstrate each of the learning outcomes specified in the assignment.

Responding positively

Assignments enable you to demonstrate what you know and how you can apply it. You should respond positively to the challenge and give it your best shot. Being well organised and having confidence in your own abilities helps too, and this is covered in the next section.

Key points

- Read instructions carefully so that you don't make mistakes that can easily be avoided, such as only doing part of the set task.
- Note the assignment deadline on your planner and any interim review dates. Schedule work around these dates to make the most of reviews with your tutor.
- Check your centre's policies relating to assignments, such as how to obtain an extension or query a final grade.
- Expect command words and/or the complexity of a task to be different at higher grades, because you have to demonstrate higher-level skills.

TOP TIP

All your assignments will relate to topics you have covered and work you have done in class. They're not meant to be a test to catch you out.

Action points

1 Check your ability to differentiate between different types of command words by doing this activity.

   a) Prepare a brief description of your usual lifestyle (pass level).

   b) Describe and justify your current lifestyle (merit level).

   c) Critically evaluate your current lifestyle (distinction level).

It would be a good idea to check that your answer is accurate and appropriate by showing it to your tutor at your next tutorial.

TOP TIP

When presenting evidence for an assessment, think about the person who will be looking through it. Plan your 'pitch' well and make it easy for the assessor to match your evidence against the grading criteria.

Sample assignment

All learners are different and will approach their assignments in different ways.
The sample assignment that follows shows how one learner answered a brief to achieve pass, merit and distinction level criteria. This learner work shows just one way in which these grading criteria can be evidenced. There are no standard or set answers. If you produce the required evidence for each task, then you will achieve the grading criteria covered by the assignment.

Front sheet

Make sure you complete the front sheet properly. Include your full name, the title of your qualification, and the unit number and name in full.

Make sure you hand in work on, or before, the deadline. It is also a good idea to ask your tutor to look through the work before you hand it in and provide feedback as to how you can improve the work.

Enter the date on which you are handing in your work. Your centre may have specific guidelines for handing in work, so make sure you know what these are before submitting the work.

This section indicates to your tutor where the work that you have produced for each criterion can be found. Some sections of your work may meet more than one criteria: if so, make sure this is clearly shown in this section.

Learner name		Assessor name
John Russell		Mrs Clara Wells

Date issued	Completion date	Submitted on
1 December 2010	3 February 2011	1 February 2011

Qualification	Unit
BTEC Level 3 National in Sport BTEC Level 3 National in Sport and Exercise Sciences	Unit 7/8: Fitness Testing for Sport and Exercise Assignment number: 3

Assignment title	Fitness Testing

In this assessment you will have opportunities to provide evidence against the following criteria. Indicate the page numbers where the evidence can be found.

Criteria reference	To achieve the criteria the evidence must show that the learner is able to:	Task no.	Page numbers
P5	Select and safely administer six different fitness tests for a selected individual recording the findings	1	1–9
M3	Justify the selection of fitness tests commenting on suitability, reliability, validity and practicality	2	observation record
P6	Give feedback to a selected individual, following fitness testing, describing the test results and interpreting their levels of fitness against normative data	3	observation record
M4	Compare the fitness test results to normative data and identify strengths and areas for improvement	3	observation record
D2	Analyse the fitness test results and provide recommendations for appropriate future activities or training	3	observation record

Learner declaration

I certify that the work submitted for this assignment is my own and research sources are fully acknowledged.

Learner signature: *John Russell*　　　　　　　　　Date: *1 February 2011*

The evidence you produce needs to meet the unit assessment and grading criteria. These are listed in this section on the assignment front sheet.

Your signature confirms that you completed the work and that it has not been copied from other sources such as a textbook, an internet site or another student.

Assignment brief

The scenario allows you to relate the assignment tasks to the real world of the sport and leisure industry.

You should always keep the assignment title in mind so that you keep focused on the main theme of the assignment.

Unit title	Unit 7/8 Fitness Testing for Sport and Exercise
Qualification	BTEC Level 3 National in Sport/Sport and Exercise Sciences
Start date	1 December 2010
Deadline date	3 February 2011
Assessor	Mrs C Wells

Assignment title	Fitness Testing

The purpose of this assignment is to:
Enable learners to gain an understanding of fitness testing procedures, test administration and how to give feedback to an individual regarding their fitness test results.

Scenario
You are working as a fitness instructor in a health and fitness club. Club members book appointments with you for fitness testing and assessment. You look in the diary and see that one person is booked in for a fitness assessment with you.

Task 1
You are to administer practical fitness tests for a selected individual.
i. Select and safely administer six different fitness tests for the individual, recording your findings on data sheets. Submit the six completed data sheets for the individual. Your assessor will also provide a witness statement.

This provides evidence for P5

Task 2
ii. During the fitness assessment you will need to justify verbally to the individual why you selected the six fitness tests you did, commenting on their suitability, reliability, validity and practicality. Your assessor will provide an observation record to confirm whether this criterion has been achieved.

This provides evidence for M3

Task 3
iii. Following fitness testing, provide verbal feedback to the individual, describing their test results, and interpret their fitness levels against normative data (P6). Use published data tables and your completed data sheets to interpret the fitness test results for the individual.
iv. During the feedback session you will need to compare the fitness test results to normative data and identify verbally the strengths and areas for improvement for the individual (M4).
v. To meet D2 you should then provide the individual with a verbal analysis of their fitness test results, offering recommendations for appropriate future activities or training.

Submit the fitness test results (completed data sheets) for the individual, together with the references for the published data tables used in the interpretation of test results. Your unit assessor will provide an observation record to confirm criteria met/not met for Task 3.

This provides evidence for P6, M4, D2

This brief has beeen verified as being fit for purpose			
Assessor	Mrs C Wells		
Signature	*Clara Wells*	**Date**	*19 November 2010*
Internal verifier	Mr I Worrell		
Signature	*Ian Worrell*	**Date**	*19 November 2010*

The tasks state what you need to do to produce evidence that meets the unit assessment and grading criteria.

These textbooks and websites have been selected to enable you to find out more about fitness testing and training, and to find research material that will support your assignment work.

Supplementary material

Sources of information

Textbooks

Adams GM – *Exercise Physiology Laboratory Manual: Health and Human Performance* (McGraw Hill Higher Education, 2001) ISBN: 9780072489125

Adams M, Barker R, Gledhill A, Lydon C, Mulligan C, Phillippo P, Sutton L – *BTEC L3 National Sport Student Book 1* (Edexcel, 2010) ISBN: 9781846906510

Adams M, Barker R, Davies W, Gledhill A, Lydon C, Mulligan C, Sergison A, Sutton L, Wilmot N – *BTEC L3 National Sport Student Book 2* (Edexcel, 2010) ISBN: 9781846906503

Adams M, Barker R, Davies W, Gledhill A, Lydon C, Mulligan C, Phillippo P, Sergison A, Sutton L – *BTEC L3 National Sport TRP* (Edexcel, 2010) ISBN: 9781846906541

Adams M, Barker R, Davies W, Gledhill A, Hancock J, Lydon C, Mulligan C, Phillippo P, Sutton L, Taylor R – *BTEC L3 National Sport and Exercise Sciences Student Book* (Edexcel, 2010) ISBN: 9781846908972

Adams M, Barker R, Davies W, Gledhill A, Hancock J, Lydon C, Mulligan C, Phillippo P, Sutton L, Taylor R – *BTEC L3 National Sport and Exercise Sciences TRP* (Edexcel, 2010) ISBN: 9781846908965

Allen MB – *Sports Exercise and Fitness: A Guide to Reference and Information Sources* (Libraries Unlimited Inc, 2005) ISBN: 9781563088193

American College of Sports Medicine – *ACSM's Guidelines for Exercise Testing and Prescription 7th edition* (Lippincott Williams & Wilkins, 2005) ISBN: 9780781745901

American College of Sports Medicine – *ACSM's Health-Related Physical Fitness Assessment Manual* (Lippincott Williams & Wilkins, 2007) ISBN: 9780781775496

Barker R et al – *BTEC National Sport: Option Units* (Heinemann, 2004) ISBN: 9780435455095

Coulson M – *The Fitness Instructor's Handbook: A Complete Guide to Health and Fitness – Fitness Professionals* (A & C Black, 2007) ISBN: 9780713682250

Franks BD, Howley ET – *Fitness Leader's Handbook* (Human Kinetics Europe, 1998) ISBN: 9780880116541

Hazeldine R – *Fitness for Sport* (The Crowood Press, 2000) ISBN: 9781861263360

Heyward VH – *Advanced Fitness Assessment and Exercise Prescription* (Human Kinetics, 2006) ISBN: 9780736057325

Honeybourne J – *BTEC National Sport: Development Coaching and Fitness* (Nelson Thornes, 2007) ISBN: 9780748781645

Howley ET, Franks BD – *Health Fitness Instructor's Handbook* (Human Kinetics Europe, 2003) ISBN: 9780736042109

National Coaching Foundation – *Physiology and Performance – NCF Coaching Handbook No 3* (Coachwise Ltd, 1987) ISBN: 9780947850241

Powers SK, Howley ET – *Exercise Physiology: Theory and Application to Fitness and Performance* (McGraw Hill Higher Education, 2006) ISBN: 9780071107266

Sharkey BJ – *Physiology of Fitness 3rd edition* (Human Kinetics, 1990) ISBN: 9780873222679

Sharkey BJ, Gaskill SE – *Fitness and Health* (Human Kinetics, 2006) ISBN: 9780736056144

Skinner J – *Exercise Testing and Exercise Prescriptions for Special Cases: Theoretical and Clinical Applications* (Lippincott Williams & Wilkins, 2005) ISBN: 9780781741132

Watson AWS – *Physical Fitness and Athletic Performance; A Guide for Students, Athletes and Coaches* (Longman, 1996) ISBN: 9780582091108

Journals

Exercise and Sport Sciences Reviews
Research Quarterly for Exercise and Sport
International Journal of Sports Science and Coaching
Medicine and Science in Sports and Exercise
American College of Sport Medicine's Health and Fitness Journal
British Journal of Sports Medicine

Useful websites for this assignment include:

British Association of Sport and Exercise Sciences	**www.bases.org.uk**
Human Kinetics	**www.humankinetics.com**
Top End Sports	**www.topendsports.com**
Sport Science	**www.sportsci.org**
Sports Coach UK	**www.sportscoachuk.org**
Coachwise	**www.1st4sport.com**
American College of Sports Medicine	**www.acsm.org**

Sample learner work

Make sure that you use a suitable pro forma to record your fitness testing results and that you record the results using the correct units, as the learner has here.

Fitness Testing

Task 1: Select and safely administer six different fitness tests for an individual, recording your findings on data sheets (P5).

The individual I have selected to participate in the fitness testing is Chris Kahlo, who also attends Ramsay College and is studying the ND in Business.

Basic Data for Chris is shown (below):

Name: Chris Jefferson Kahlo
Age: 17 years
Height: 1.79 m
Weight: 80 kg

At the start, I spoke to Chris about what fitness tests he would be interested in doing, and took this into account, so I know that the results are going to be of use and interest to him. Chris told me he is particularly interested in finding out what his aerobic fitness is like and also his body fat, because he's training at the moment to try and tone up. Chris enjoys running and cycling, and wants to push himself hard in the tests, so this also helped me with the test selection, because I wanted to try and make sure the tests would be specific and suitable for him. Knowing what Chris was interested in has helped me with the selection of six different fitness tests.

The six different fitness tests I will administer for Chris are:
1. Sit and reach test (for flexibility)
2. Multi-stage fitness test (for VO_2 max – aerobic endurance, which is what Chris was interested in finding out)
3. Wingate test (for anaerobic power, Chris likes cycling)
4. Skinfold testing (for percent body fat, Chris was interested in finding out his result)
5. Grip dynamometer (for handgrip strength)
6. 35m sprint test (for speed)

I have completed a data sheet for each test, showing Chris's results.

It is good practice to carry out multiple tests. In this case the learner undertook two tests, followed by a re-test.

Ramsay College of FE

Sit and Reach Test

Name: Chris Kahlo   Date: 07.12.2010

Gender: Male

Wt = 80 kg

Ht = 1.79 m

Trial 1 = 13 cm
Trial 2 = 13 cm
Average = 13 cm

Re-test (same day):
Trial 1 = 14 cm
Trial 2 = 14 cm
Average = 14 cm

Units of measurement = cm

Notes: *We used a sit-and-reach box (Cranlea Medical).*

The results of the multi-stage fitness test have been converted into ml per kg per minute. This shows a full understanding of how the test score relates to VO_2 max.

It is good practice to list the equipment you used and your data sources.

Ramsay College of FE

Multi-stage Fitness Test

Name: Chris Kahlo

Gender: male

Trial 1 Result: Level 9 Shuttle 11 = VO_2 max = 46.8 ml/kg/min   Date: 10.12.2010

Trial 2 Result: Level 10 Shuttle 4 = VO_2 max = 48.0 ml/kg/min   Date: 15.12.2010

Notes: *A data table was used to look up the VO_2 max result (ml/kg/min) from the level and shuttle Chris reached. Equipment – multi-stage fitness test audiotape, tape recorder, 4 cones, 2 people acted as spotters.*

This learner has tabulated the results, displaying them clearly.

Ramsay College of FE

Wingate Anaerobic Cycle Test Data Sheet 1

Name: Chris Kahlo   Date: 12.01.2011

Gender: male

Body weight = 80 kg

Weight to add to basket   = body weight x 0.075
                                                    = 6 kg
– 1 kg for the basket weight   = 6 – 1
                                                    = 5 kg basket weight

Time (s)	RPM
5	118
10	118
15	115
20	114
25	109
30	106

Calculation of Chris's anaerobic power:

Time (s)	Anaerobic Power (W)
5	$6 \times (118/60 \times 5) \times 11.765 = 694.1\,W$
10	$6 \times (118/60 \times 5) \times 11.765 = 694.1\,W$
15	$6 \times (115/60 \times 5) \times 11.765 = 676.5\,W$
20	$6 \times (114/60 \times 5) \times 11.765 = 670.6\,W$
25	$6 \times (109/60 \times 5) \times 11.765 = 641.2\,W$
30	$6 \times (106/60 \times 5) \times 11.765 = 623.5\,W$

Peak anaerobic power result = 694.1 W

Working out has been provided to show how the fatigue rate has been predicted. This is good practice.

Ramsay College of FE

Wingate Anaerobic Cycle Test Data Sheet 2

Name: Chris Kahlo

Date: 12.01.2011

Anaerobic capacity (kgm–30s)

= total revs in 30s × 6m × Force (kg)
= 57 × 6 × 6
= 2052 (kgm–30s)

Workings to show total revs for Chris:

Time (s)	5s revs	
5	118/60 × 5	9.83
10	118/60 × 5	9.83
15	115/60 × 5	9.58
20	114/60 × 5	9.50
25	109/60 × 5	9.08
30	106/60 × 5	8.83
Total revs	56.65 = 57 (closest rev)	

Anaerobic capacity (W)

= kgm–30 s/3
= 2052/3
= 684 W (average mean power)

Calculation of power decline:

$$100 \times \frac{(\text{peak anaerobic power} - \text{low anaerobic power})}{\text{peak anaerobic power}} = \% \text{ fatigue rate}$$

$$= 100 \times \frac{(694.1 - 623.5)}{694.1} = 10.17 \% \text{ fatigue rate}$$

Before any testing, an informed consent form should be signed by the participant. It is included here as evidence that this pre-test procedure was followed.

Wingate Anaerobic Cycle Test

Informed Consent Form

1. The purpose of the test is to determine maximal anaerobic power and maximal anaerobic capacity.
2. This will be determined using the Wingate anaerobic cycling test.
3. The subject will carry out standard warming-up and cooling-down procedures. For warm-up, the subject will need to cycle for between 2 and 4 minutes at an intensity sufficient to cause the heart to beat at 150–160 bpm. Cycling during the warm-up will need to include two or three all-out bursts of cycling for 4–8 seconds each. For cool-down, and to minimise risk of fainting, the subject will need to cycle with no load on the basket, for 2–3 minutes after the test. The subject will be given help to get off the bike and should then assume the instructed recovery position, as a precaution.
4. The subject will be required to perform a 30-second all-out cycling test using a Monark 824E cycle ergometer.
5. The subject will receive method details in full. Due to the stressful nature of this test, the test will not be repeated. If a re-test is required, this will be held on a separate day.
6. The tester is available to answer any relevant queries which may arise concerning the test.
7. The subject is free to withdraw consent and discontinue participation in the test at any time.
8. Recorded data will be treated confidentially.

I fully understand the scope of my involvement in this test. I fully understand the arduous nature of this test and have freely consented to be a subject.

Subject signature: *Chris Kahlo*　　　　Date: *07 January 2011*
Tester signature: *John Russell*　　　　Date: *07 January 2011*
Parent/Guardian signature: *F Kahlo (Mrs)*　　　Date: *07 January 2011*

Equations have been included that clearly show how the percent body fat has been calculated.

Ramsay College of FE

Skinfold Testing

Name: Chris Kahlo   Date: 14.01.2011

Gender: male

Age: 17 years

Skinfold site	Chest (mm)	Abdomen (mm)	Thigh (mm)
Trial 1	6.2	12	12.2
Trial 2	7	11	12
Average	6.6	11.5	12.1

Results using J–P calculations:
SSF = Sum of chest, abdomen and thigh (mm)
Body density (Bd) = $1.1093800 - (0.0008267 \times SSF) + (0.0000016 \times (SSF^2)) - (0.0002574 \times \text{age in years})$

$$
\begin{aligned}
Bd \quad &= 1.1093800 - (0.0008267 \times 30.2) + (0.0000016 \times 912.04) - (0.0002574 \times 17) \\
&= 1.1093800 - (0.0249663) + (1.45926 \times 10^{-3}) - (4.3758 \times 10^{-3}) \\
&= 1.0844137 + 1.45926 \times 10^{-3} - 4.3758 \times 10^{-3} \\
&= 1.08
\end{aligned}
$$

Calculation of percent body fat (Brozek, 1959):
$$
\begin{aligned}
\% \text{ body fat} &= [(4.57/\ Bd) - 4.142] \times 100 = \% \text{ fat} \\
&= [(4.57/1.08) - 4.142] \times 100 = \% \text{ fat} \\
&= [0.089] \times 100 = 8.95 \ \% \text{ body fat}
\end{aligned}
$$

Notes: *The Jackson & Pollock skinfold method for males was used, which was chest, abdomen and thigh. Equipment – I used Harpenden skinfold calipers, a tape measure and a pen to mark the sites.*

Three trials on each hand have been carried out, with an average taken for each hand. The best results have then been reported.

Ramsay College of FE

Individual Data for Handgrip Strength

Name: Chris Kahlo   Date: 14.01.2011

Gender: male

Age: 17 years

(kg)	Trial 1	Trial 2	Trial 3	Average
Right	43	40	44	42
Left	47	48	49	48
Right	44	45	44	44
Left	48	48	49	48
Right	44	44	45	44
Left	48	49	50	49

Results:
Best right hand = 45 kg
Best left hand = 50 kg
We used a manual handgrip dynamometer (takei Kiki Kogyo)

The learner has tabulated and correctly interpreted the overall results from the six fitness tests. Assessment criterion P5 has been achieved.

Ramsay College of FE

35m Sprint Test Data Sheet

Name: Chris Kahlo   Date: 17.01.2011

Gender: male

Age: 17 years

Trial Number	Time (s)
1	5.20
2	5.10

The test was performed in the college sports hall. Chris had a 5-minute recovery period between trial 1 and trial 2.

OVERALL FITNESS TEST RESULTS FOR CHRIS KAHLO

Fitness component	Fitness test	Trial 1	Trial 2	Test result	Units	Interpretation of test results (Rating)
Flexibility	Sit-and-reach test	13	14	14	cm	Average
Aerobic endurance (VO$_2$ max)	Multi-stage fitness test	46.8	48	48	ml/kg/min	Good
Anaerobic power	Wingate test	694.1	-	694.1	W	Average
Body composition	Skinfold testing	8.95	-	8.95	% Body fat	Slim
Strength	Handgrip strength	44 (R) 48 (L)	44 (R) 49 (L)	45 (R) 50 (L)	kg	Average (R) Good (L)
Speed	35m sprint	5.2	5.1	5.1	s	Average

Remember to reference any sources you have used. This shows you have done your research and avoids plagiarism issues.

Sample learner work: page 10

Learner name: John Russell

Assignment references

Bar-Or O (1978); *A New Anaerobic Capacity Test: Characteristics and Applications.* Proceedings of the 21st World Congress in Sports Medicine. Brasilia.

Brozek J (1959); *Techniques for Measuring Body Composition.* Quartermaster Research Engineering Centre (AD<286506) Natick, Mass, p95.

Hueger WWK (1989); *Sit and Reach Test Tables.* Lifetime Physical Fitness and Wellness. Morton Publishing.

Inbar O, Bar-Or O (1986); *Anaerobic Characteristics in Male Children and Adolescents.* Medicine and Science in Sports and Exercise, 18 (3): 264–269.

Jackson AS, Pollock ML (1978); *Generalised Equations for Predicting Body Density of Men.* British Journal of Nutrition, 40, 497–504.

Leger LA, Lambert J (1982); *A Maximal Multistage 20m Shuttle Run Test to Predict VO_2 max.* European Journal of Applied Physiology, 49, 1–5.

Police Force Fitness Assessment Mark Sheet.

Sharkey B.J (1990); *Physiology of Fitness.* Human Kinetics, Champaign, Illinois.

The University of Loughborough, Department of Physical Education and Sports Science (1987); *Table of Predicted Maximum Oxygen Uptake Values for the Multistage Fitness Test.*

Witness statement

> A witness statement can be used to confirm that the fitness tests were selected, safely administered and results recorded. This statement confirms that assessment criterion P5 has been met.

Learner name	John Russell
Qualification	BTEC Level 3 National in Sport BTEC Level 3 National in Sport and Exercise Sciences
Unit number and title	Unit 7/8: Fitness Testing for Sport and Exercise

Description of activity undertaken (please be as specific as possible)

- Selection of six different fitness tests for an individual
- Safe administration of each test

Assessment and grading criteria

P5: Select and safely administer six different fitness tests for a selected individual recording the findings

Evidence is sufficient to support achievement of assessment criterion P5.

How the activity meets the requirements of the assessment and grading criteria, including how and where the activity took place

Six different fitness tests administered to selected individual (C Kahlo). These were:
Sit and reach test (07.12.2010); multi-stage fitness test (10.12.2010); anaerobic Wingate test (12.01.2011); skinfold testing (14.01.2011); handgrip dynamometer (14.01.2011); 35 m sprint test (17.01.2011).

Tests were administered either in the College sports hall, gym or classroom. Learner took the individual's age, general sports ability and personal needs into account when selecting suitable tests. Correct test methodology was adhered to closely throughout. Pre-test procedures were followed. The individual to be tested was fully briefed on test protocols. Learner was aware of reasons for test termination, and was watchful of this, particularly for the more physically stressful test administered (Wingate) and informed consent obtained. Health, safety and welfare of the subject considered throughout.

Witness name	N/A	Job role	N/A	
Witness signature	N/A		Date	N/A
Learner name	John Russell			
Learner signature	John Russell		Date	17 January 2011
Assessor name	Mrs C Wells			
Assessor signature	Clara Wells		Date	17 January 2011

Observation record

The observation record provides evidence to show that your assessor observed you carrying out the six different fitness tests. It needs to be signed by you and your assessor to confirm that these activities actually took place and confirm the assessment criterion achieved (P5).

Learner name	John Russell

Qualification	BTEC Level 3 National in Sport BTEC Level 3 National in Sport and Exercise Sciences

Unit number and title	Unit 7/8: Fitness Testing for Sport and Exercise

Description of activity undertaken (please be as specific as possible)

Six fitness tests were selected and administered for a chosen individual

Task 2:
- Verbal justification to the individual of why each fitness test was selected (M3).

Task 3:
- Verbal feedback to the individual following each fitness test and interpretation of test results against normative data (P6).
- Verbal identification of the individual's strengths and areas for improvement (M4).
- Verbal analysis of the individual's fitness test results, providing recommendations for appropriate future activities or training (D2).

Assessment and grading criteria

M3: Justify the selection of fitness tests, commenting on suitability, reliability, validity and practicality

P6: Give feedback to a selected individual, following fitness testing, describing the test results and interpreting their levels of fitness against normative data

M4: Compare the fitness test results to normative data and identify strengths and areas for improvement

D2: Analyse the fitness test results and provide recommendations for appropriate future activities or training

Have these assessment and grading criteria been achieved? – YES, criteria M3, P6, M4 and D2 have been met.

How the activity meets the requirements of the assessment and grading criteria

M3: At start of first fitness testing session (flexibility sit and reach test – 07.12.2010), learner provided verbal justification to the individual, discussing tests selected and why these had been chosen. Learner took into account the individual's age, sports ability and interests to select tests that would be suitable. This included selecting a physically stressful test (Wingate) because the individual stated he was a keen cyclist and wanted to work to his max. Learner discussed test validity and reliability issues for each test, covering aspects such as use of re-tests, ensuring an all-out effort and the importance of keeping in time with bleeps on the multi-stage fitness test. Test practicality was discussed, including disadvantages of maximal and sub-maximal tests and how this had affected test selection. Learner justified the greater usefulness of sport-specific tests selected (ie running – multi-stage fitness test and cycling – Wingate test), because these would better reflect the physiological demands of the individual's sport and specific working muscles. **M3 – MET**

P6: Six fitness tests were administered to the selected individual between 07.12.2010 and 17.01.2011. Following each test, the learner used published data tables to interpret the individual's test results and comprehensive feedback was provided regarding their fitness levels. All results were recorded accurately using data collection sheets. **P6 – MET.**

M4: Learner compared each test result to published data tables according to the individual's age, gender and ethnic origin and verbally identified the strengths and areas for improvement. **M4 – MET.**

D2: After completing the final fitness test (35m sprint test – 17.01.2011), learner provided an overall verbal analysis of the six test results and recommended appropriate future activities and training methods. This included use of hill sprints, hollow sprints and fartlek training to develop speed. Interval training for developing aerobic fitness and plyometric circuits, which learner stated could be tailored to be sport-specific. PNF stretching discussed, although individual was not interested in incorporating this into his training regime. **D2 – MET.**

Learner signature	*John Russell*		Date	*17 January 2011*
Assessor signature	*Clara Wells*		Date	*17 January 2011*
Assessor name	Mrs C Wells			

Assessor's comments

Detailing what you enjoyed and any problems that you experienced will help you in future assignments. It may also help your tutor revise the assignment, and this could help learners in the future.

This section shows if you have achieved each criteria – 'Y' is yes and 'N' is no.

Qualification	BTEC Level 3 National in Sport/ Sport and Exercise Sciences	Year	2010–11
Unit number and title	7/8: Fitness Testing for Sport and Exercise – Assignment 3	Learner name	John Russell

Grading criteria	Achieved?
P5 Select and safely administer six different fitness tests for a selected individual recording the findings	Y
M3 Justify the selection of fitness tests commenting on suitability, reliability, validity and practicality	Y
P6 Give feedback to a selected individual following fitness testing, describing the test results and interpreting their levels of fitness against normative data	Y
M4 Compare the fitness test results to normative data and identify strengths and areas for improvement	Y
D2 Analyse the fitness test results and provide recommendations for appropriate future activities or training	Y

Learner feedback

I enjoyed this assignment because it gave me the opportunity to use fitness testing skills I picked up on the First Diploma in Sport, and this time administer tests for another individual. I also thought it was good that it was basically all practical work, because I don't like writing reports much, it can be a bit boring. Chris enjoyed finding out what his fitness levels were like and how these could be improved.

Assessor feedback

This is an excellent piece of work John. You have performed extremely well throughout, showing your professional, mature and confident manner. You adhered closely to standard test protocols, ensuring the health, safety and welfare of your subject throughout. Witness statement and observation record provided to confirm achievement of practically based assessment and grading criteria. Very well done.

Action plan

It's good practice to include references in text where appropriate (as well as in your overall references section). For future assignments, you could use several data interpretation tables for each test (they do vary!), to build up a wider picture of the fitness testing results obtained.

Assessor signature	Clara Wells	Date	10 February 2011
Learner signature	John Russell	Date	15. February 2011

The action plan shows what you need to do to improve the assignment that has just been assessed (if required) and what you should focus on in future assignments. It is an important tool that you can use to improve your work.

The assessor has provided this learner with useful feedback that highlights his strengths and areas for improvement.

Step Seven: Work productively as a member of a group

Case study: Team relationships

David is 17 years old and has recently started work in a leisure centre as a pool lifeguard and leisure assistant. He worked and trained hard to get his lifeguard qualification, and this hard work paid off as he passed the national pool lifeguard qualification on his first attempt. He now works shifts at the weekend and the occasional evening. He is also studying for the BTEC Level 3 National in Sport qualification during the week.

David is finding the travel aspect of the job more difficult than he had thought. He doesn't have a car and the leisure centre is too far away for him to walk. His early shift on a Saturday starts at 6 am, and buses do not run very frequently at that time of day. If he misses the bus, he has to wait over half an hour for the next one. This means that he arrives around 30 minutes late for the early shift. The other members of staff in his team have to cover his initial tasks, such as cleaning the changing rooms prior to opening up, while trying to do their own work. This does not make David too popular with the other staff.

David has little experience of setting up sports equipment such as badminton courts and five-a-side football goals, so he tries to avoid that aspect of his job. However, this means that the other staff have to set up the equipment, and the job takes much longer than it should.

David has never completed any courses in customer care and does not know how to react when clients have a complaint.

Reflection point

In each of the situations described in this case study, what do you think David should do in order to improve his relationship with the rest of the team and make his supervisor happy with his work?

In your private life, you can choose your own friends, whereas at work you are paid to work alongside many people, whether you like them or not. This applies at school or college too. Hopefully, by now, you've outgrown wanting to only work with your best friends on every project.

You may not be keen on everyone in your team, but you should still be pleasant and co-operative. This may be harder if you are working with a partner than in a large group.

Sometimes you may be the group leader. This may inspire you, or fill you with dread. You won't be expected to develop team-leader skills overnight, but it helps if you know the basics.

First, you should understand how groups and teams work and why good teamwork is considered vital by employers.

Working in groups and teams

If you have a full-time or part-time job, you already belong to a working group, or team. At school or college your class is an example of a working group.

All working groups have some common characteristics:

- doing the same type of work – though in the workplace you probably have different roles or responsibilities
- a group leader or supervisor
- a reason for working together, such as studying for the same qualification or tackling an area of work too large for someone to do alone
- group members are dependent on each other in some way; at work you may have to cover someone's workload if they are absent
- group members concentrate on their individual achievements and success.

A team is different. As a team member you have a specific objective to achieve **together** – and this is more important than the goals of individual team members.

TOP TIP

Understanding how groups and teams function will help you be a better team worker and a better team leader.

These are the characteristics of a team.

- Team members have a team goal which is more important than any personal goals.
- Team members have complementary skills so that the team can achieve more than individuals working alone could achieve.
- Work is allocated to play to each person's strengths and talents.
- The team members give each other encouragement and support.
- There is collective responsibility for achieving the goal.

A good team leader acts as facilitator and motivator, and gives practical support and guidance.

Working in a team has many benefits. Team members can learn from each other and combine their skills to do a better job more quickly. Working with other people is often more enjoyable than working alone, too. Many industries rely heavily on efficient group working, from IT teams to health workers and the emergency services.

TOP TIP

Focusing on the task rather than on personalities is the first step in learning to work with different people whose views may not match your own.

There are many benefits to be gained from working as a team.

Being a good team member

Everyone wants team members who are talented, positive, cheerful and full of energy. These are the key areas to focus on if you wish to be a good team member.

- **Your social skills.** This includes being courteous, treating other people as you wish to be treated, saying 'please' when you want something, and thanking people who do you a favour.

- **Your temperament**. Expect people to have different views and opinions from you, and don't take offence if someone disagrees with you. If you lose your temper easily, learn to walk away before you say something you may regret.

- **Your communication skills.** This includes talking and listening!

Practise saying what you mean clearly, accurately and succinctly. Be prepared to give good reasons to justify your arguments and ideas.

Allow people to finish what they're saying, without interruption, before you talk. Never shout people down. Think before you speak so that you don't upset people with tactless remarks. If you inadvertently do so, apologise.

- **Your commitment.** Always keep your promises and never let anyone down when they are depending upon you. Always do your fair share of the work, even if you don't agree with all the decisions made by your team. Tell people promptly if you are having problems so there is time to solve them. Be loyal to your team when you're talking to other people.

Being the team leader

It can be difficult to strike a balance between leading the team and working with friends. You need to inspire and motivate your team without being bossy or critical.

Important points to remember about being a team leader

- Lead by example. Stay pleasant, consistent and control your temper, even under pressure.
- Everyone is different. Your ways of working may not always be the best.
- Be prepared to listen and contribute positively to a discussion.
- Encourage quieter team members to join in discussions by asking for their views.
- Be prepared to do whatever you ask other people to do.
- Note down what you say you will do, so that you don't forget.
- Discuss alternatives with people rather than giving orders.
- Be sensitive to other people's feelings. They may have personal problems or issues that affect their behaviour.
- Learn the art of persuasion.
- Act as peacemaker. Help people reach a compromise when necessary.
- Give team members the credit for their hard work or good ideas.
- Admit your mistakes. Look for a positive solution and think about what can be learned for the future, rather than making excuses.
- Praise and encourage team members who are working hard.
- Make criticisms constructively, and in private.
- Be assertive (put forward your point of view firmly) rather than aggressive (attacking other people to defend yourself).

Some notes of caution about being a team leader

- Try to look pleasant and don't glare at people who interrupt you unexpectedly.
- Never talk about team members behind their backs.
- Don't gossip, exaggerate to make a point, spread rumours, speculate or tell lies.
- Don't expect to get your own way all the time – all good leaders back down on occasion.
- Never criticise any colleagues in front of other people. Speak to them in private and keep it constructive.

TOP TIP

Excellent ideas often come from quiet team members. Encourage everyone to make suggestions so that you don't overlook any valuable contributions.

Key points

- There are many benefits of working in a group or as a team. These include mutual support, companionship and the exchange of ideas.
- You will be expected to work co-operatively with other people at work, and during many course assignments.

- It isn't easy learning to be a team leader. Team leaders should be fair, consistent and pleasant to work with, as well as loyal and sensitive to the needs of team members.

Action points

1 Identify the role of teamwork in your area of study. Identify the team's goal and any factors you think will contribute towards its success.

2 Decide how you would handle each of the following difficult situations if you were the team leader. If you can, discuss your ideas with a friend in your class.
   a) The team needs to borrow a college video camera to record an event being held tonight. Your tutor tells you that the one you reserved last week is not working and the rest are out on loan.
   b) A member of your team has personal problems so you have given him less work to do. Now you've been accused of having favourites.
   c) A team member is constantly letting everyone down because of poor work and non-attendance at group meetings.
   d) Two team members have disagreed about how to do a task. You're not bothered how they do it as long as it gets done properly, and by the deadline.
   e) A team member becomes very aggressive whenever she is challenged in any way – no matter how mildly.

3 Identify someone who has inspired you because they've been an excellent leader. This could be someone you've met, a fictional character or a famous person. Note down what it is about them that impressed you.

TOP TIP

Team working and bouncing ideas around produce quicker and better results than working in isolation.

Activity: Teamwork in the sports industry

The types of career available in the sports industry usually require people to work as a team member or as the team leader (and sometimes both at the same time), so it is essential that you develop the necessary skills.

Explain how you would be expected to work as a member of a team in the following situations that occur regularly in the sports industry.

- Setting up a fitness circuit

- Cleaning changing rooms

- Checking gym equipment at the start of the day

- Getting safety equipment ready for a kayaking expedition

- Assisting a person who has been injured

- Dealing with a customer complaint

Step Eight: Understand how to research and analyse information

Case study: Using and analysing research to find a job

Julie is at a sixth form centre studying for a BTEC Level 3 National Diploma in Sport and Exercise Sciences. She is in school for four and a half days a week, and she wants to try and find some part-time work for the occasional evening and weekends. She wants to try to earn some money to help with the running costs of her car. She also wants to gain some useful work experience which will help her in the future to get other work in the sport and active leisure industry.

She does not want to travel too far to work, so she is only really looking for job opportunities in the local area. Julie is looking at many websites to help with her search for work. (Go to page 98 to find out how to look at the websites that Julie monitors.)

These websites give her information on what sorts of jobs are available, details about the job role, and an idea of the sort of salary she could expect from each job.

Julie also looks through local newspapers to see if any jobs are being advertised that aren't also on the internet sites she monitors.

When she is happy with the amount of information she has gathered, Julie creates a three-column table. In the left-hand column she lists each job that might be suitable for her, in the centre column all the things in favour of each job, and in the last column all the things against it. This helps her organise the information she has gathered and to make decisions about what she wants to do.

Reflection points

Do you think Julie's system would work for you? How would you go about organising and analysing this kind of information?

As a BTEC Level 3 National learner, you often have to find information for yourself. This skill will be invaluable in your working life and if you continue your studies at higher education level. Sometimes the information will give you a better understanding of a topic, at other times you will research information for a project or assignment. Sometimes you may be so interested in something that you want to find out more without being told to do so!

Whatever your reason, and no matter where your information can be found, there is a good and not-so-good way to go about the task. This section will help if you can't find what you want, or find too much, or drift aimlessly around a library, or watch a demonstration and don't know what to ask afterwards.

Types of information

There are many types of information and many different sources. Depending on the task, these are the sources you may need to consult.

- **Verbal information.** This includes talking to friends, colleagues at work and members of your family, listening to experts explain what they do, interviewing people, talking to sales reps at an exhibition or customers about a product.
- **Printed information.** This includes information printed in newspapers, journals, magazines, books, posters, workshop manuals, leaflets and catalogues. The type of magazine or newspaper you read may have its own slant on the information, which you may have to take into account.
- **Written information.** This includes course notes and handouts, reports, and other documents in the workplace. If you want to use written information from work, you must check that this is allowed and that it doesn't contain confidential material such as financial information or staff names and addresses.
- **Graphical information.** This includes illustrations, pictures, cartoons, line drawings, graphs and photographs. Graphics can make something clearer than words alone. For example, a satnav instruction book might contain illustrations to show different procedures.
- **Electronic information.** This includes information from electronic sources such as DVDs, CD-ROMs, searchable databases, websites, podcasts, webinars (**seminars** online), emails and text messages. The huge amount of information available online is both a help and a hindrance. You can find information quickly, but the source may be unreliable, out of date, inaccurate or inappropriate (see page 66.)

TOP TIP

Too much information is as bad as too little, because it's overwhelming. The trick is to find good-quality, relevant information and know when to call a halt to your search.

TOP TIP

Consider all appropriate sources and don't just rely on information found online.

Finding what you need

Spend a few minutes planning what to do before you start looking for information. This can save a lot of time later on.

The following steps will help you to do this.

1 Make sure you understand exactly what it is you need to know so that you don't waste time looking for the wrong thing.

2 Clarify your objectives to narrow down your search. Think about why the information is wanted and how much detail you need. For example, learners studying BTEC Nationals in Engineering and Performing Arts may both be researching 'noise' for their projects, but they are likely to need different types of information and use it in different ways.

3 Identify your sources and check you know how to use them. You need to choose sources that are most likely to provide information relevant to your objectives. For example, an engineering learner might find information on noise emissions in industry journals and by checking out specialist websites.

4 Plan and schedule your research. Theoretically, you could research information forever. Knowing when to call a halt takes skill. Write a schedule that states when you must stop looking and start sorting the information.

5 Store your information safely in a labelled folder. This folder should include printouts or photocopies of articles, notes about events you have attended or observed, photographs you've taken or sketches you've drawn. Divide your information under topic headings to make it easier to find. When you're ready to start work, re-read your assignment brief and select the items that are most closely related to the task you are doing.

Allocate time for research as part of your assignment task. Take into account any interim deadlines as well as the final deadline for completing the work.

Primary and secondary research, and the law of copyright

There are two ways to research information. One is known as primary research, the other is secondary research.

Primary research

Primary research involves finding new information about an issue or topic. This might include finding out people's views about a product or interviewing an expert. When carrying out interviews, you will need to design a survey or questionnaire. Your primary research might also include observing or experiencing something for yourself, and recording your feelings and observations.

Secondary research

Secondary research involves accessing information that already exists in books, files and newspapers or on CD-ROMs, computer databases or the internet, and assessing it against your objectives.

This information has been prepared by other people and is available to anyone. You can quote from an original work provided you acknowledge the source of your information. You should put this acknowledgement in your text or in the bibliography to your text; do not claim it as your own research. You must include the author's name, year of publication, the title and publisher, or the web address if it is an online article. You should practise listing the sources of articles so

that you feel confident writing a bibliography. Use the guidance sheet issued by your centre to help you. This will illustrate the style your centre recommends. (See also page 68.)

The trick with research is to choose the best technique to achieve your objectives, and this may mean using a mix of methods and resources. For example, if you have to comment on an industry event you might go to it, make notes, interview people attending, observe the event (perhaps take a video camera), and read any newspaper reports or online comments.

Always make sure you make a note of where you get information from (your source). Keep it safely as it can be very difficult later on to work out where it came from!

People as a source of information

If you want to get the most out of interviewing someone or several people, you need to prepare carefully in advance.

The following points give some general advice about getting the most out of face-to-face interviews.

- Make sure you know what questions to ask to get the information you need.
- Explain why you want the information.
- Don't expect to be told confidential or sensitive information.
- Write clear notes so that you remember who told you what, and when. (See also page 68.)
- Note the contact details of the person you are interviewing and ask whether they mind if you contact them again should you think of anything later or need to clarify your notes.
- Thank them for their help.

If you want to ask a lot of people for their opinion, you may want to conduct a survey. You will need to design a questionnaire and analyse the results. This will be easier if you ask for **quantitative** responses – for example yes/no, true/false or ratings on a five-point scale – rather than opinions.

- Give careful thought to your representative sample (people whose opinions are relevant to the topic).
- Decide how many people to survey so that the results mean something.
- Keep the survey relatively short.
- Thank people who complete it.
- Analyse the results, and write up your conclusions promptly.

TOP TIP

Test your questionnaire on volunteers before you 'go live' to check that there are no mistakes and that the questions are easy to understand. Make any amendments before you conduct your 'real' survey.

Asking someone who knows a lot about a topic can be informative.

Avoiding pitfalls

Wikipedia is a good online source that covers many topics, and often in some depth. It is popular and free. However, it has an open-content policy, which means that anyone can contribute to and edit entries. People may post information whether it is correct or not. Wikipedia is moving towards greater checks on entries, but it is still sensible to check out information you find on this site somewhere else.

Apart from inaccuracy, there are other problems that you may find with any information you obtain through research, especially material found online.

- **Out-of-date material.** Check the date of everything and keep only the latest version of books, newspapers or magazines. Yesterday's news may be of little use if you are researching something topical.
- **Irrelevant details.** Often, only part of an article will be relevant to your search. For example, if you are forecasting future trends in an area of work, you do not need information about its history or related problems. When learners are struggling, they sometimes 'pad out' answers with irrelevant information. If you've researched properly you can avoid this by having enough relevant information for your purposes.

- **Invalid assumptions.** This means someone has jumped to the wrong conclusion and made 2 + 2 = 5. You might do this if you see two friends chatting and think they are talking about you – whether they are or not! You can avoid problems in this area by double-checking your ideas and getting evidence to support them.

- **Bias.** This is when people hold strong views about a topic, or let their emotions or prejudices affect their judgement. An obvious example is asking a keen football fan for an objective evaluation of their team's performance!

- **Vested interests.** People may argue in a certain way because it's in their own interests to do so. For example, when the government said Home Information Packs must be prepared for all properties being sold, the Association of Home Information Pack Providers was in favour because it trains the people who prepare the packs. The National Association of Estate Agents and Royal Institution of Chartered Surveyors were not, because they thought they would lose business if people were put off selling their houses.

TOP TIP

Don't discard information that is affected by bias or vested interests. Just make it clear you know about the problem and have taken it into account.

Reading for a purpose

You may enjoy reading or you may find it tedious or difficult. If so, it helps to know that there are different ways to read, depending on what you're doing. For example, you wouldn't look for a programme in a TV guide in the same way that you would check an assignment for mistakes. You can save time and find information more easily if you use the best method of reading to suit your purpose. The following are some examples of ways of reading.

- **Skim reading** is used to check new information and get a general overview. To skim a book chapter, read the first and last paragraphs, the headings, subheadings and illustrations. It also helps to read the first sentence of each paragraph.

TOP TIP

News articles are written with the key points at the beginning, so concentrate on the first paragraph or two. Feature articles have a general introduction and important information is contained in the main text.

- **Scanning** is used to see whether an article contains something you need – such as key words, dates or technical terms. Focus on capital or initial letters for a name, and figures for a date. Technical terms may be in bold or italics.

- **Light reading** is usually done for pleasure when you are relaxed, for example, reading a magazine article. You may not remember many facts afterwards, so this sort of reading isn't suitable for learning something or assessing its value.

- **Word-by-word reading (proofreading)** is important so that you don't miss anything, such as the dosage instructions for a strong medicine. You should proofread assignments before you submit them.

- **Reading for study (active reading)** means being actively involved so that you understand the information. It is rare to be naturally good at this, so you might have to work to develop this skill.

Developing critical and analytical skills

Developing critical and analytical skills involves looking at information for any flaws in the arguments. These skills are important when you progress to work or higher education (HE), so it's useful to practise them now on your BTEC Level 3 National course.

A useful technique for understanding, analysing, evaluating and remembering what you are reading is **SQ4R**.

SQ4R is an effective method. It consists of six steps.

1 Survey first, to get a general impression. Scan the information to see what it is about, when it was written and by whom. The source, and the reason it was written, may be important. Most newspapers, for example, have their own 'slant' that affects how information is presented.

2 Question your aims for reading this material. What are you hoping to find? What questions are you expecting it to answer?

3 Read the information three or four times. The first time, aim to get a general idea of the content. Use a dictionary to look up any new words. Then read more carefully to really understand what the writer means.

4 Respond by thinking critically about the information and how it relates to the topic you are studying. Does it answer your queries partially, fully or not at all? What information is factual and what is based on opinion? Is there evidence to support these opinions? Is there a reason why the author has taken this standpoint? Do you agree with it? How does it link to other information you have read? What is the opposite argument and is there any evidence to support this? Overall, how useful is this information?

5 Record the information by noting the key points. Use this to refresh your memory, if necessary, rather than re-reading the article.

6 Review your notes against the original to check you have included all important points. If you are also preparing a presentation, reviewing your notes will help you to remember key points more easily.

TOP TIP

SQ4R is just one method of reading for study. Research others and adapt them to suit your own style.

Taking good notes

There are many occasions when you need to take notes, such as when a visiting speaker is talking to your class. There's no point taking notes unless you write them in a way that will allow you to use them later.

Note-taking is a personal activity. Some people prefer to make diagrammatical sketches with key points in boxes linked by arrows, others prefer to write a series of bullet points. You will develop your own style, but the following hints and tips might help you at the start.

- Use A4 lined paper, rather than a notebook, so that you have more space and don't need to turn over so often.
- When you're reading for study, make sure you have a dictionary, pen, notepad and highlighter to hand.
- Leave a wide margin to record your own comments or queries.
- Put a heading at the top, such as the speaker's name and topic, as well as the date.
- If you are making notes from a book or an article, remember SQ4R and read it several times first. Your notes will only be effective if you understand the information.
- Don't write in complete sentences – it takes too long.
- Leave spaces for later additions or corrections.
- Use headings to keep your notes clear and well organised.
- Only write down relevant information, including key words and phrases.

- Highlight, underline or use capitals for essential points.
- Never copy chunks of text – always use your own words.
- Clearly identify quotations, and record your sources, so that you can cite them in your work. (Note the author's name, title, publisher, date and place of publication and the page number.)

TOP TIP

Make sure your information is accurate, up to date, relevant and valid. Be aware of bias, and don't confuse fact with opinion.

Key points

- Useful information may be verbal, printed, written, graphical or electronic.
- Effective research means knowing exactly what you are trying to find and where to look. Know how reference media are stored in your library and how to search online. Store important information carefully.
- Primary research is original data you obtain yourself. Secondary research is information prepared by someone else. If you use this, you must quote your sources in a bibliography.
- You can search for information by skimming and scanning, and read in different ways. Reading for study means actively involving yourself with the text, questioning what you are reading and making notes to help your own understanding.
- Read widely around a topic to get different viewpoints. Don't accept everything you read as correct. Think about how it fits with other information you have obtained.
- Taking notes is a personal skill that takes time to develop. Start by using A4 lined pages with a margin, set out your notes clearly and label them. Only record essential information.

Action points

- Working with a friend, look back at the sources of information listed on page 64. For each type, identify examples of information relevant to your course that you could obtain from each source. See how many you can list under each type.
- Check your ability to find the information you need by answering each of the questions in **Activity: Finding information** on the next page. For any questions you get wrong, your first research task is to find out the correct answers as quickly as you can.
- Go to page 98 to find out how you can access a website where you can check your ability to skim and scan information, improve your ability to differentiate fact from opinion, summarise text, and much more.
- Check your ability to sort fact from opinion and spot vested interests by completing **Activity: Let's give you a tip…** on page 72. Check your ideas with the answers on page 97.

TOP TIP

Make a note of any information that you are struggling to understand so that you can discuss it with your tutor.

Activity: Finding information

Answer the following questions about finding information.

a) Four types of information that are available from the library in your centre, besides books, are:

1

2

3

4

b) When I visit the library, the way to check if a book I want is available is:

c) The difference between borrowing a book on short-term loan and on long-term loan is:

Short-term loan:

Long-term loan:

d) The journals that are stocked by the library that are relevant to my course include:

e) Useful information on the intranet at my centre includes:

f) Searchable databases and online magazines I can access include:

g) The quickest way to check if a book or journal contains the type of information I need is to:

h) The difference between a search engine, a portal, a directory site and a forum is:

i) Bookmarking useful websites means:

j) In addition to suggesting websites, Google can also provide the following types of information:

k) Specialist websites which provide useful information related to my course include:

l) Useful tips I would give to people starting on my course who need to find out information are:

Activity: Let's give you a tip...

In 2009 many businesses were struggling, thanks to the credit crunch and falling consumer demand. Some, like Woolworths, closed down altogether. Others laid off staff, or announced wage cuts. Despite this, the government approved recommendations by the Low Pay Commission to increase the minimum wage rate from October. Although the rise was only small, many unions, including Unison and Usdaw, agreed it was better than a freeze, which had been wanted by the British Chambers of Commerce and the British Retail Consortium.

The government also announced new laws to stop restaurants and bars using tips to top up staff pay to the minimum level. *The Independent* newspaper claimed its 'fair tips, fair pay' campaign had won the day. It also reported that the British Hospitality Association was claiming this could result in up to 45,000 job losses. The Unite union also carried out a campaign, and its General Secretary claimed the decision a triumph for the poorly paid. Not everyone agreed. Some thought there should be no tipping at all, as in Australia. Others said the Canadian system was best – wages are low but generous tips are left, and this motivates staff to give excellent service.

a) Look at the table below. In your view, which of the statements are facts and which are opinions? In each case, justify your view.

Statement	Fact or opinion?	Justification
i) Having a national minimum wage helps low-paid workers.		
ii) Over one million people will benefit from the minimum wage increase.		
iii) The new law on tips will stop restaurants paying below minimum wage rates.		
iv) Using the Australian system of no tips would be better.		
v) The Canadian system guarantees good service.		
vi) 45,000 job losses will occur in the hospitality industry.		

b) All newspapers have their own way of putting forward the news. Go to page 98 to find out how you can access a website which will help you to compare the way that news is reported in different newspapers.

Compare six different newspapers and make notes on:

i) the type of stories covered

ii) the way views are put forward.

Activity: A quick look at fitness tests

Fitness tests are used to assess the different components of individual fitness and to devise training programmes to improve levels of fitness. They are an important research method in sport, and a means of gathering primary data for analysis.

A group of five adults are tested for body composition (body mass index – BMI). The BMIs (in kg/m²) of the five people in the group are:

a 22   d 28

b 21   e 17

c 18

Look at the following table and determine which category each person in the test falls into. Discuss the results, the implications for health and fitness, and any issues affecting the validity of this classification.

BMI (kg/m²)	Classification
< 18.5	underweight
18.5–24.9	normal weight
25.0–29.9	overweight
30.0–34.9	class I obesity
35.0–39.9	class II obesity
≥ 40.0	class III obesity

Source: World Health Organization (2000)

Another group of young people participate in a test for flexibility (sit and reach test).

There are five men and five women in the group. These are the test results.

Men (cm)	Women (cm)
25	30
16	18
-11	12
8	0
27	-9

Use the internet to search for how these results are rated. A particularly useful website can be accessed via www.pearsonhotlinks.co.uk. Go to page 98 to find out how to access it.

What is the average sit and reach score for the men and what is the average score for the women?

How do these scores compare with the ones you have found online?

What two training methods could performers undertake to improve their body mass index, and what training methods would improve their flexibility?

Step Nine: Make an effective presentation

Case study: Making an effective presentation

Stephen has to deliver a presentation on nutrition in sport for an assignment. While he really enjoys the subject, he has never given a presentation before. He is very nervous at the prospect of delivering a presentation but sets about his work. He spends time carrying out research to make sure that he has sufficient information on the subject. He then needs to put this into a presentation format.

Stephen has learned how to use PowerPoint software to produce the presentation. He has some top tips which he follows to help him deliver a good presentation.

- He only puts the main points he wants to cover on each slide, and he then talks around the subject in the presentation. This avoids putting too many words on a slide.
- He tries to include some drawings and photographs on his slides to help illustrate the points he is making.
- He practises the presentation with the slides, so he has everything arranged in the correct order. This avoids the possibility that he may show one slide while attempting to cover the content on another slide. This also helps him to improve the flow of his presentation and keep to his allotted time.

Once his PowerPoint presentation is ready, Stephen makes notes on flash cards. He prepares one flash card for each slide.

He then practises delivering his presentation in his bedroom. After two or three trial runs, he times himself to check that the presentation lasts between 10 and 15 minutes. He then practises the presentation in front of his mum, which helps him to get used to speaking in front of an audience.

When it comes to delivering his presentation in front of his tutor, Stephen has few nerves as he has put in enough preparation and practice. The tutor asks him a few questions at the end, and Stephen is pleased that he is able to answer each question.

Stephen receives the highest grade he can get for this assignment, and he now feels much less worried at the prospect of delivering another presentation.

Reflection points

How will you prepare for presentations that you have to give on your BTEC course?

Making a presentation can be nerve-wracking. It involves several skills, including planning, preparation and communication. It tests your ability to work in a team, speak in public and use IT (normally PowerPoint). You also have to stay calm under pressure. However, as it is excellent practice for your future, you can expect presentations to be a common method of assessing your performance.

TOP TIP

When you're giving a presentation, keep to time, get to the point and use your time well.

Good planning and preparation

Being well prepared, and rehearsing beforehand, helps your confidence and your presentation. The following points will help you to do this.

- If you're part of a team, find out everyone's strengths and weaknesses and divide work fairly, taking these into account. Decide how long each person should speak, who should introduce the team and who will summarise at the end.
- Take into account the time you have been allocated, your resources and team skills. A simple, clear presentation is better – and safer – than a complicated one.

- If you're using PowerPoint, make slides more interesting by avoiding a series of bulleted lists and including artwork. Print PowerPoint notes for the audience. Use a fuller set of notes for yourself, as a prompt.
- Check the venue and time.
- Decide what to wear and check it's clean and presentable.
- Prepare, check and print your handouts.
- Decide, as a team, the order in which people will speak, bearing in mind the topic.
- Discuss possible questions and how to answer them.
- Rehearse beforehand to check your timings.

If you prepare properly, you can really enjoy giving a presentation.

TOP TIP

Rehearsing properly allows you to speak fluently, just glancing at your notes to remind you of the next key point.

On the day, you can achieve a better performance if you:

- arrive in plenty of time
- calm your nerves by taking deep breaths before going in front of your audience
- introduce yourself clearly, and smile at the audience
- avoid reading from your screen or your notes
- explain what you are going to do – especially if giving a demonstration – do it, and then review what you've done
- say you will deal with questions at the end of any demonstration
- answer questions honestly – don't exaggerate, guess or waffle
- respond positively to all feedback, which should be used to improve your performance next time.

TOP TIPS

Make sure you can be heard clearly by lifting your head and speaking a little more slowly and loudly than normal.

Key points

- When making a presentation, prepare well, don't be too ambitious, and have several rehearsals.
- When giving a demonstration, explain first what you are going to do and that you will answer questions at the end.

Case study: Learner quotes about making presentations

Most people start off feeling uncomfortable about talking in front of a group of people, whether you know them or not. This is what some real learners have said about having to give presentations as part of their BTEC course.

'I used to dread presentations on my course, but found that if I went through my notes again and again until I knew the presentation inside out, it made it much easier and the presentations generally went well.'

Javinder, 17, BTEC Level 3 National in Construction

'I used to be petrified of talking in front of other people but over time I've learned that, if I prepare well before a presentation, I usually feel much more confident on the day. If I know my material, I don't have to look down at my notes all the time and can make eye contact with the audience. Taking a few deep breaths before I begin keeps me calm and allows me to focus.'

Katie, 19, BTEC Level 3 National in Creative Media Production

'I used to hate presenting to other people on my course, until I realised that most of them were as nervous about it as I was!'

Koichi, 21, BTEC Level 3 National in Art and Design

'Less is more! I used to rely on props and, as I was nervous about forgetting things or running out of things to say, I talked far too quickly. I had to repeat everything as nobody knew what I was on about! Some of my best presentations have been done without using slides or any other props at all, just talking (slowly of course) to my audience.'

Laura, 18, BTEC Level 3 National in Health & Social Care

'I prefer to be assessed by oral presentations as I'm dyslexic and my written work lets me down all the time. Everyone tells me that I really shine and show that I know my stuff when I present it to the rest of the group.'

Sam, 17, BTEC Level 3 National in Business

Activity: All right on the night?

Read the following account and answer the questions that follow.
If possible, compare ideas with a friend in your class.

Gemma looked around in exasperation. The team were on the final rehearsal of their presentation and nothing was going right. Amaya seemed to think it was funny. 'Honestly, Gemma, why don't you just chill for a bit?' she suggested. 'You know what they say – a bad dress rehearsal means we'll do really well tomorrow!'

Gemma glared at her. 'Well, can I make a suggestion, too, Amaya,' she retorted. 'Why don't you just concentrate for a change? Sprawling around and dissolving into giggles every five minutes isn't helping either.'

She turned to Adam. 'And I thought you were going to build a simple model,' she said, 'not one that falls apart every time you touch it.'

Adam looked crest fallen. 'But I wanted to show how it worked.'

'How it's supposed to work, you mean!' raged Gemma, all her worries and anxieties now coming to the fore. 'We'll look stupid if it ends up in bits on the floor tomorrow and Amaya just falls about laughing again.'

'And Imran,' continued Gemma, turning her sights on the last member of the team, 'why is it so difficult for you to count to three minutes? We've agreed over and over again we'll each talk for three minutes, and every time you get carried away with the sound of your own voice and talk for twice as long. It just means we're going to overrun and get penalised. And stop trying to wriggle out of answering questions properly. For heaven's sake, if you don't know the answer, how hard is it just to say so?'

Silence fell. No one looked at each other. Adam fiddled with his model and something else fell off. Amaya wanted to laugh but didn't dare.

Imran was sulking and vowed never to say anything ever again. 'You wait,' he thought. 'Tomorrow I'll race through my part in one minute flat. And then what are you going to do?'

1 Identify the strengths and weaknesses of each member of the presentation team.

Name	Strengths	Weaknesses
Gemma		
Amaya		
Adam		
Imran		

2 What have the team done right, so far, in getting ready for their presentation?

3 Why do you think they are having problems?

4 If you were Gemma's tutor, what advice would you give her at this point?

Activity: Preparing for a presentation

Select a sport and prepare a presentation that describes:

- why you enjoy this sport
- the benefits of playing the sport
- the players (or role models) that you admire
- why the sport appeals to many people.

Carry out research on your selected sport. You could use the internet, textbooks, newspapers and journals to help you with your research.

Use the slide plans below to note the content and design the layout for each slide. Think about how you can best present the information you have compiled from your research. Try to illustrate your talk. For example, if you are making a presentation about football, you could include photos of well-known football players. Your illustrations should help emphasise the points you are making. Note, you do not have to actually deliver the presentation – just design each slide.

3

4

5

6

TOP TIP

When making a PowerPoint presentation, don't just read out what it says on the slides. The audience can do this. Use the slides as prompt cards.

Step Ten: Maximise your opportunities and manage your problems

Case study: Maximise your opportunities

Mark is on the second year of his BTEC Level 3 National in Sport (Performance and Excellence) course. He has done very well in his first year, and he wants to do as well as he can in his second year so that he can go on to higher education and continue his studies in sport. Mark is a keen football player and has been playing for both his local club and his school team for over six years.

Mark was spotted by a talent scout, and he has been asked to train and compete with a semi-professional football club in his area. Mark is very pleased, and he has given some thought about how his training commitments and match days can be helpful towards the completion of assignment tasks. He has made some notes on how he should follow this up.

- Talk to the coaches to gain information about different types of training programmes.
- Review and discuss elite sports performers with the coaches and trainers to find out about their training regimes, physical and psychological characteristics, and other attributes.

- Ask the coaches to provide witness statements to confirm I have taken part in activities relevant to my course, such as participation in a training session, completion of a training programme, leading a training session with peers, designing a training session and coaching others.
- Design a training programme for a team-mate, and maintain regular contact to monitor progress and to evaluate the programme.
- Review own performance, identifying strengths and areas for improvement.
- Review the performance of others and provide feedback.

Reflection points

What additional evidence or information could you obtain through your sporting commitments to use in completing your assignments?

If your course takes one or two years to complete, then it is highly likely that you will experience some highs and lows in that time. You may find one or two topics harder than the rest. There may be distractions in your personal life to cope with. All of this means that you may not always be able to do your best.

It is, therefore, sensible to have an action plan to help you cope. It's also wise to plan how to make the best of opportunities for additional

experiences or learning. This section shows you how to do this.

TOP TIP

Because life rarely runs smoothly, it's sensible to capitalise on the opportunities that come your way and have a plan to deal with problems.

Making the most of your opportunities

There will be many opportunities for learning on your course, not all of which will be in school or college. You should prepare for some of the following to maximise the opportunities that each offers.

- **External visits**. Prepare in advance by reading about relevant topics. Make notes when you are there. Write up your notes neatly and file them safely for future reference.

- **Visiting speakers**. Questions can usually be submitted to the speaker in advance. Think carefully about information that you would find helpful. Make notes, unless someone has been appointed to make notes for the whole group. You may be asked to thank the speaker on behalf of your group.

- **Work experience**. If work experience is an essential part of your course, your tutor will help you to organise your placement and tell you about the evidence you need to obtain. You may also get a special logbook in which to record your experiences. Read and re-read the units to which your evidence will apply, and make sure you understand the grading criteria and what you need to obtain. Make time to write up your notes, logbook and/or diary every night (if possible), while everything is fresh in your mind.

- **In your own workplace**. If you have a full-time or part-time job, watch for opportunities to find out more about relevant topics that relate to your course, such as health and safety, teamwork, dealing with customers, IT security and communications. Your employer will have had to address all of these issues. Finding out more about these issues will broaden your knowledge and give more depth to your assessment responses.

- **Television, newspapers, podcasts and other information sources**. The media can be an invaluable source of information. Look out for news bulletins relating to your studies, as well as information in topical television programmes – from *The Apprentice* to *Top Gear*. You can also read news headlines online (see page 73). Podcasts are useful, too. It will help if you know what topics you will be studying in the months to come, so you can spot useful opportunities as they arise.

TOP TIP

Remember that you can use online catch-up services, such as the BBC iPlayer or 4oD (for Channel 4 shows) to see TV programmes you have missed recently.

Minimising problems

Hopefully, any problems you experience during your course will only be minor, such as struggling to find an acceptable working method with someone in your team.

You should already know who to talk to about these issues, and who to go to if that person is absent or you would prefer to talk to someone else. If your problems are affecting your work, it's sensible to see your tutor promptly. It is a rare learner who is enthusiastic about every topic and gets on well with everyone else doing the course, so your tutor won't be surprised and will give you useful guidance (in confidence) to help.

TOP TIP

Don't delay talking to someone in confidence if you have a serious problem. If your course tutor is unavailable, talk to another staff member you like and trust instead.

Other sources of help

If you are unfortunate enough to have a more serious personal problem, the following sources of help may be available in your centre.

- **Professional counselling.** There may be a professional counselling service. If you see a counsellor, nothing you say during the session can be mentioned to another member of staff without your permission.

- **Complaint procedures.** If you have a serious complaint, the first step is to talk to your tutor. If you can't resolve your problem informally, there will be a formal learner complaint procedure. These procedures are used only for serious issues, not for minor difficulties.

- **Appeals procedures.** If you disagree with your final grade for an assignment, check the grading criteria and ask the subject tutor to explain how the grade was awarded. If you are still unhappy, talk to your personal tutor. If you still disagree, you have the right to make a formal appeal.

- **Disciplinary procedures.** These exist for when learners consistently flout a centre's rules, and ensure that all learners are dealt with in the same way. Hopefully, you will never get into trouble, but you should make sure that you read these procedures carefully to see what could happen if you did. Remember that being honest and making a swift apology is always the wisest course of action.

- **Serious illness.** Whether this involves you, a family member or a close friend, it could affect your attendance. Discuss the problem with your tutor promptly; you will be missing information from the first day you are absent. There are many solutions in this type of situation – such as sending notes by post and updating you electronically (providing you are well enough to cope with the work).

TOP TIP

It's important to know your centre's procedures for dealing with important issues such as complaints, major illnesses, learner appeals and disciplinary matters.

Key points

- Don't miss opportunities to learn more about relevant topics through external visits, listening to visiting speakers, work experience, being at work or even watching television.
- If you have difficulties or concerns, talk to your tutor, or another appropriate person, promptly to make sure your work isn't affected.

Action points

1 Prepare in advance to maximise your opportunities.
   a) List the opportunities available on your course for obtaining more information and talking to experts. You can check with your tutor to make sure you've identified them all.
   b) Check the content of each unit you will be studying so that you know the main topics and focus of each.
   c) Identify the information that may be relevant to your course on television, on radio, in newspapers and in podcasts.

2 Make sure you know how to cope if you have a serious problem.
   a) Check your centre's procedures so you know who to talk to in a crisis, and who to contact if that person is absent.
   b) Find out where you can get hold of a copy of the main procedures in your centre that might affect you if you have a serious problem. Then read them.

Activity: Dealing with problems

During your BTEC Level 3 National in Sport or Sport and Exercise Sciences you may, at some time, encounter a problem. You can maximise your opportunities by being prepared for this possibility by making notes on who to contact and what to do if specific problems arise.

1 Complete this table with the information that applies to your centre.

Who should I contact if …	Person to contact and what to do
I am off ill?	
I have a problem with any of my work?	
I have a personal problem?	
I don't agree with the grade I have been given for one of my assignments?	
I am in trouble for something, such as lateness, not handing in work, poor attendance or plagiarism?	

2 You will probably go on some visits during your course. You might visit places involved with sport. This can be really useful as you will get to see how different parts of the sports industry work and some of the career opportunities that may be open to you. Answer these questions to help you prepare for a visit to a leisure centre.

- Is there anything that I should take with me on the visit?
- What information should I collect?
- How should I collect this information?
- How will I use this information (for which units and assignment tasks)?

AND FINALLY …

Refer to this Study Skills Guide whenever you need to remind yourself about something related to your course. Keep it in a safe place so that you can use it whenever you need to refresh your memory. That way, you'll get the very best out of your course – and yourself!

TOP TIP

The time and effort you will be putting into this course deserve to be rewarded. Make sure you know how to confront and successfully overcome problems.

Skills building

This section has been written to help you improve the skills needed to do your best in your assignments. You may be excellent at some skills already, others may need further work. The skills you can expect to demonstrate on your course include:

- your personal, learning and thinking skills (**PLTS**)
- your **functional skills** of ICT, maths/numeracy and English
- your proofreading and document production skills.

Personal, learning and thinking skills (PLTS)

These are the skills, personal qualities and behaviour that enable you to operate more independently, work more confidently with other people and be more effective at work. You'll develop these on your BTEC Level 3 National course through a variety of experiences and as you take on different roles and responsibilities.

The skills are divided into six groups.

1 **Independent enquirers** can process and evaluate information they investigate from different perspectives. They can plan what to do and how to do it, and take into account the consequences of making different decisions.

2 **Creative thinkers** generate and explore different ideas. They make connections between ideas, events and experiences that enable them to be inventive and imaginative.

3 **Reflective learners** can assess themselves and other people. They can evaluate their own strengths and limitations. They set themselves realistic goals, monitor their own performance and welcome feedback.

4 **Team workers** collaborate with other people to achieve common goals. They are fair and considerate to others, whether as a team leader or team member, and take account of different opinions.

5 **Self-managers** are well-organised and show personal responsibility, initiative, creativity and enterprise. They look for new challenges and responsibilities, and are flexible when priorities change.

6 **Effective participators** play a full part in the life of their school, college, workplace or wider community by taking responsible action to bring improvements for others as well as themselves.

Action points

1 Many parts of this Study Skills Guide relate to the development of your own personal, learning and thinking skills. For each of the following, suggest the main skill groups to which the chapter relates. Refer to the box above and write a number next to each chapter title below.

a) Use your time wisely. ____

b) Understand how to research and analyse information. ____

c) Work productively as a member of a group. ____

d) Understand yourself. ____

e) Utilise all your resources. ____

f) Maximise your opportunities and manage your problems. ____

2 You have been on your BTEC National course for a few months now and, although everyone is enjoying the work, you realise that some of the learners have complaints.

First, several learners object to an increase in the price of printouts and photocopying, on the basis that they can't do good work for their assignments if this is too expensive. You disagree and think that the prices are reasonable, given the cost of paper.

Second, a timetable change means your 2 pm – 4 pm Friday afternoon class has been moved to 9 am – 11 am. Some learners are annoyed and want it changed back, while others are delighted.

a) For the first problem, identify four factors which could indicate that those complaining about the price rise might be justified.

1

2

3

4

b) Now consider the second problem.

i) Think about which learners in your group would be most affected by the timetable change. Who might be most disturbed? Who might benefit from the earlier start?

ii) Try to think of a creative solution, or compromise, that would please both groups.

c) During the discussions about these issues, some quieter members of the class are often shouted down by the more excitable members. Suggest a strategy for dealing with this which everyone is likely to accept.

You can also check your ideas with the suggestions given on page 97.

3 a) Complete the chart opposite, identifying occasions when you may need to demonstrate personal, learning and thinking skills in your future career. Alternatively, apply each area to a part-time job you are currently doing.

b) Identify areas where you think you are quite strong and put a tick in the 'S' column. Check that you could provide evidence to support this judgement, such as a time when you have demonstrated this skill.

c) Now consider areas where you are not so good and put a cross in the 'W' column.

d) Then practise self-management by identifying two appropriate goals to achieve over the next month and make a note of them in the space provided. If possible, talk through your ideas at your next individual tutorial.

Personal, learning and thinking skills for future career/current part-time job				
Skill group	Example skills	Occasions when you use/ will use skill	S	W
Independent enquirers	Finding information			
	Solving problems			
	Making decisions			
	Reconciling conflicting information or views			
	Justifying decisions			
Creative thinkers	Finding imaginative solutions			
	Making original connections			
	Finding new ways to do something			
	Opportunities for being innovative and inventive			
Reflective learners	Goals you may set yourself			
	Reviewing your own progress			
	Encouraging feedback			
	Dealing with setbacks or criticism			
Team workers	Working with others			
	Coping with different views from your own			
	Adapting your behaviour			
	Being fair and considerate			
Self-managers	Being self-starting and showing initiative			
	Dealing positively with changing priorities			
	Organising your own time and resources			
	Dealing with pressure			
	Managing your emotions			
Effective participators	Identifying issues of concern to others			
	Proposing ways forward			
	Identifying improvements for others			
	Influencing other people			
	Putting forward a persuasive argument			
Goals	1			
	2			

Functional skills

Functional skills are practical skills that everyone needs to have in order to study and work effectively. They involve using and applying English, maths and ICT.

Improving your literacy skills

Your written English communication skills

A good vocabulary increases your ability to explain yourself clearly. Work that is presented without spelling and punctuation errors looks professional, and increases the likelihood of someone understanding your intended meaning. Your written communication skills will be tested in many assignments. You should work at improving areas of weakness, such as spelling, punctuation or vocabulary.

Try the following ideas to help you improve your written communication skills.

- Read more as this introduces you to new words, and it will help your spelling.
- Look up new words in a dictionary and try to use them in conversation.
- Use a thesaurus (you can access one electronically in Word) to find alternatives to words you use a lot; this adds variety to your work.
- Never use words you don't understand in the hope that they sound impressive.
- Write neatly, so people can read what you've written.
- Do crosswords to improve your word power and spelling.
- Improve your punctuation – especially the use of apostrophes – either by using an online programme or by using a communication textbook.
- Go to page 98 to find out how to gain access to some helpful websites for this page.

Verbal and non-verbal communication (NVC) skills

Talking appropriately means using the right words and 'tone'; using the right body language means sending positive signals to reinforce this message – such as smiling at someone when you say 'Hello'. Both verbal and non-verbal communication skills are essential when dealing with people at work.

The following ideas are some hints for successful communication.

- Be polite, tactful, and sensitive to other people's feelings.
- Think about the words and phrases that you like to hear, and use them when communicating with other people.
- Use simple language so that people can understand you easily. Explain what you mean, when necessary.
- Speak at the right pace. Don't speak so slowly that everyone loses interest, or so fast that no one can understand you.
- Speak loudly enough for people to hear you clearly – but don't shout!
- Think about the specific needs of different people – whether you are talking to a senior manager, an important client, a shy colleague or an angry customer.
- Recognise the importance of non-verbal communication (NVC) so that you send positive signals by smiling, making eye contact, giving an encouraging nod or leaning forwards to show interest.
- Read other people's body language to spot if they are anxious or impatient so that you can react appropriately.

TOP TIP

Make sure you use the right tone for the person you're talking to. Would you talk to an adult in the same way you'd talk to a very young child?

Action points

1 Go to page 98 to find out how to gain access to websites which can help you to improve your literacy skills.

2 A battery made in China contained the following information.

> **DO NOT CONNECT IMPROPERLY**
>
> **CHARGE OR DISPOSE OF IN FIRE**

a) Can you see any problems with this? Give a reason for your answer.

b) Reword the information so that it is unambiguous.

3 If you ever thought you could completely trust the spellchecker on your computer, type the text given in box A on the next page into your computer. Your spellchecker will not highlight a single error; yet even at a glance you should be able to spot dozens of errors!

Read the passage in box A and try to understand it. Then rewrite it in box B on the next page without spelling, grammatical or punctuation errors. Compare your finished work with the suggested version on page 97.

Box A

Anyone desirable to write books or reports, be they short or long, should strive too maximise they're optimal use of one's English grammar and obliviously there is an need for correct spelling two one should not neglect punctuation neither.

Frequent lea, many people and individuals become confusing or just do not no it, when righting, when words that mean different, when sounding identically, or when pronounced very similar, are knot too bee spelled inn the same whey. The quay two suck seeding is dew care, a lack off witch Leeds too Miss Spellings that mite otherwise of bean a voided. Spell chequers donut find awl missed takes.

Despite all the pitfalls how ever, with practise, patients and the right altitude, any one can soon become a grate writer and speaker, as what I did.

Box B Now rewrite the passage in the space below without errors.

4 In each of the statements listed in the table below suggest what the body language described might mean.

Statement	What might this body language mean?
a) You are talking to your manager when he steps away from you and crosses his arms over his chest.	
b) You are talking to your friend about what she did at the weekend but she's avoiding making eye contact with you.	
c) During a tutorial session, your tutor is constantly tapping his fingers on the arm of his chair.	
d) Whenever you talk to your friend about your next assignment, she bites her lower lip.	

Improving your maths or numeracy skills

If you think numeracy isn't relevant to you, then think again! Numeracy is an essential life skill. If you can't carry out basic calculations accurately then you will have problems, perhaps when you least expect them. You'll often encounter numbers in various contexts – sometimes they will be correctly given, sometimes not. Unless you have a basic understanding about numeracy, you won't be able to tell the difference.

Good numeracy skills will improve your ability to express yourself, especially in assignments and at work. If you have problems, there are strategies that you can practise to help:

- Try to do basic calculations in your head, then check them on a calculator.
- Ask your tutor for help if important calculations give you problems.
- When you are using your computer, use the onscreen calculator (or a spreadsheet package) to do calculations.
- Investigate puzzle sites and brain training software, such as Dr Kageyama's Maths Training by Nintendo.

Action points

1 Go to page 98 to find out how to gain access to websites which can help you to improve your numeracy skills.

2 Try the following task with a friend or family member.

Each of you should write down 36 simple calculations in a list, eg

8×6, $19 - 8$, $14 + 6$.

Exchange lists. See who can answer the most calculations correctly in the shortest time.

3 Figures aren't always what they appear to be. For example, Sophie watches *Who Wants To Be a Millionaire?* She hears Chris Tarrant say that there have been over 500 shows, with 1200 contestants who have each won over £50,000 on average. Five people have won £1 million.

Sophie says she is going to enter because she is almost certain to win more than £50,000 and could even win a million pounds.

a) On the figures given, what is the approximate total of money won over 500 shows (to the nearest £ million)?

b) Assuming that Sophie is chosen to appear on the show, and makes it on air as a contestant, do you think Sophie's argument that she will 'almost certainly' win more than £50,000 is correct? Give a reason for your answer.

(The correct answer is on page 98.)

4 You have a part-time job and have been asked to carry out a survey on the usage of the drinks vending machine. You decide to survey 500 people, and find that:

- 225 use the machine to buy one cup of coffee per day only
- 100 use the machine to buy one cup of tea per day only
- 75 use the machine to buy one cup of cold drink per day only
- 50 use the machine to buy one cup of hot chocolate per day only
- the rest are non-users
- the ratio of male to female users is 2:1.

a) How many men in your survey use the machine?

b) How many women in your survey use the machine?

c) Calculate the proportion of the people in your survey that use the machine.

Express this as a fraction and as a percentage.

d) What is the ratio of coffee drinkers to tea drinkers in your survey?

e) What is the ratio of coffee drinkers to hot chocolate drinkers in your survey?

f) If people continue to purchase from the machine in the same ratio found in your survey, and last month 1800 cups of coffee were sold, what would you expect the sales of the cold drinks to be?

g) Using the answer to f), if coffee costs 65p and all cold drinks cost 60p, how much would have been spent in total last month on these two items?

Improving your ICT skills

Good ICT skills are an asset in many aspects of your daily life and not just for those studying to be IT practitioners.

These are ways in which you can improve your ICT skills.

- Check that you can use the main features of the software packages you need to produce your assignments, eg Word, Excel and PowerPoint.

- Choose a good search engine and learn to use it properly. For more information, go to page 98 to find out how to access a useful website.

- Developing and using your IT skills enables you to enhance your assignments. This may include learning how to import and export text and artwork from one package to another; taking digital photographs and inserting them into your work, and/or creating drawings or diagrams by using appropriate software.

Action points

1 Check your basic knowledge of IT terminology by identifying each of these items on your computer screen:

a) taskbar

b) toolbar

c) title bar

d) menu bar

e) mouse pointer

f) scroll bars

g) status bar

h) insertion point

i) maximise/ minimise button.

2 Assess your IT skills by identifying the packages and operations you find easy to use and those that you find more difficult. If you use Microsoft Office products (Word, PowerPoint, Access or Excel) you can find out more about improving your skills online. Go to page 98 to find out how to access a useful website for this action points section.

3 Search the internet to find a useful dictionary of IT terms. Bookmark it for future use. Find out the meaning of any of the following terms that you don't know already:

a) portal

b) cached link

c) home page

d) browser

e) firewall

f) HTML

g) URL

h) cookie

i) hyperlink

j) freeware.

Proofreading and document preparation skills

Improving your keyboard, document production and general IT skills can save you hours of time. When you have good skills, the work you produce will be of a far more professional standard.

- Think about learning to touch-type. Your centre may have a workshop you can join, or you can use an online program – go to page 98 to find out how to access a web link for this section. From here you can access websites that will allow you to test and work on improving your typing skills.

- Obtain correct examples of any document formats you will have to use, such as a report or summary, either from your tutor, from the internet or from a textbook.

- Proofread all your work carefully. A spellchecker won't find all your mistakes, so you must read through it yourself as well.

- Make sure your work looks professional by using a suitable typeface and font size, as well as reasonable margins.

- Print your work and store the printouts neatly, so that it stays in perfect condition for when you hand it in.

Action points

1 You can check and improve your typing skills using online typing sites – see link in previous section.

2 Check your ability to create documents by scoring yourself out of 5 for each of the following questions, where 5 is something you can do easily and 0 is something you can't do at all. Then focus on improving every score where you rated yourself 3 or less.

I know how to:

a) create a new document and open a saved document _____

b) use the mouse to click, double-click and drag objects _____

c) use drop-down menus _____

d) customise my toolbars by adding or deleting options _____

e) save and/or print a document _____

f) create folders and sub-folders to organise my work _____

g) move a folder I use regularly to My Places _____

h) amend text in a document _____

i) select, copy, paste and delete information in a document _____

j) quickly find and replace text in a document _____

k) insert special characters _____

l) create a table or insert a diagram in a document _____

m) change the text size, font and colour _____

n) add bold, italics or underscore _____

o) create a bullet or numbered list _____

p) align text left, right or centred _____

q) format pages before they are printed _____

r) proofread a document so that there are no mistakes _____.

Answers

Activity: Let's give you a tip... (page 72)

a) i) Fact

ii) Opinion – the number cannot be validated

iii) Fact

iv) Opinion

v) Opinion

vi) Opinion – again the number is estimated

Skills building answers

PLTS action points (page 87)

1 a) Use your time wisely = **5** Self-managers

b) Understand how to research and analyse information = **1** Independent enquirers, **5** Self-managers

c) Work productively as a member of a group = **4** Team workers, **6** Effective participators

d) Understand yourself = **3** Reflective learners

e) Utilise all your resources = **5** Self-managers

f) Maximise your opportunities and manage your problems = **1** Independent enquirers, **2** Creative thinkers, **3** Reflective learners, **5** Self-managers

2 a) Factors to consider in relation to the increased photocopying/printing charges include: the comparative prices charged by other schools/colleges, how often there is a price rise, whether any printing or photocopying at all can be done without charge, whether there are any concessions for special tasks or assignments, the availability of class sets of books/popular library books for loan (which reduces the need for photocopying).

b) i) An earlier start will be more likely to negatively affect those who live further away and who are reliant on public transport, particularly in rural areas. The earlier finish will benefit anyone who has a part-time job that starts on a Friday afternoon or who has after-college commitments, such as looking after younger sisters or brothers.

ii) The scope for compromise would depend on whether there are any classes between 11 am and 2 pm on a Friday, whether tutors had any flexibility and whether the new 9 am – 11 am class could be moved to another time or day.

c) One strategy would be to allow discussion for a set time, ensure everyone has spoken, then put the issue to a vote. The leader should prompt suggestions from quieter members by asking people individually what they think.

Literacy skills action points (page 91)

2 a) The statement reads as if it is acceptable to either charge it or dispose of it in fire.

b) Do not connect this battery improperly. Do not recharge it and do not dispose of it in fire.

3 Anyone who wishes to write books or reports, whether short or long, should try to use English grammatically. Obviously there is a need for correct spelling, too. Punctuation should also not be neglected.

Frequently, people confuse words with different meanings when they are writing, especially when these sound identical or very similar, even when they must not be spelled in the same way. The key to succeeding is due care, a lack of which leads to misspellings that might otherwise have been avoided. Spellcheckers do not find all mistakes.

Despite all the pitfalls, however, with practice, patience and the right attitude, anyone can soon become a great writer and speaker, like me.

4 Possible answers.

a) Stepping backwards and crossing arms across the chest might indicate that your manager is creating a barrier between you and himself. This may be because he is angry with you.

b) Your friend may be feeling guilty about what she did at the weekend, or not confident that you will approve of what she tells you.

c) Your tutor might be frustrated as he has many things to do and so wants the tutorial to finish quickly.

d) Your friend might be anxious about the next assignment or about the time she has to complete it.

Numeracy action points (page 94)

3 a) £60 million

b) Sophie's argument is incorrect as £50,000 is an average, some contestants will win more, but many will win much less. The distribution of prize money is greater at lower amounts because more people win small amounts of money than large amounts – and only five contestants have won the top prize of £1 million.

4 a) 300

b) 150

c) 9/10ths, 90%

d) 225:100 (= 45:20) = 9:4

e) 225:50 = 9:2

f) 600

g) £1530

Accessing website links

Links to various websites are referred to throughout this BTEC Level 3 National Study Skills Guide. To ensure that these links are up to date, that they work and that the sites aren't inadvertently linked to any material that could be considered offensive, we have made the links available on our website: www.pearsonhotlinks.co.uk. When you visit the site, search for either the title BTEC Level 3 National Study Skills Guide in Sport or ISBN 9781846906596. From here you can gain access to the website links and information on how they can be used to help you with your studies.

Useful terms

Accreditation of Prior Learning (APL)
Some of your previous achievements and experiences may be able to be used to count towards your qualification.

Apprenticeships
Schemes that enable you to work and earn money at the same time as you gain further qualifications (an NVQ award and a technical certificate) and improve your functional skills. Apprentices learn work-based skills relevant to their job role and their chosen industry. See page 98 for how you can access a website to find out more.

Assessment methods
Techniques used to check that your work demonstrates the learning and understanding required for your qualification, such as assignments, case studies and practical tasks.

Assessor
An assessor is the tutor who marks or assesses your work.

Assignment
A complex task or mini-project set to meet specific grading criteria and learning outcomes.

Awarding body
An organisation responsible for devising, assessing and issuing qualifications. The awarding body for all BTEC qualifications is Edexcel.

Credit value
The number of credits attached to your BTEC course. The credit value increases in relation to the length of time you need to complete the course, from 30 credits for a BTEC Level 3 Certificate, 60 credits for a Subsidiary Diploma, 120 credits for a Diploma, up to 180 credits for an Extended Diploma.

Degrees
Higher education qualifications offered by universities and colleges. Foundation degrees take two years to complete; honours degrees may take three years or longer.

Department for Business Innovation and Skills (BIS)
BIS is responsible for further and higher education and skills training, as well as functions related to trade and industry. See page 98 for how you can access a website to find out more.

Department for Education
The Department for Education is responsible for schools and education, as well as children's services. See page 98 for how you can access a website to find out more.

Distance learning
When you learn and/or study for a qualification at home or at work. You communicate with your tutor and/or the centre that organises the course by post, by telephone or electronically.

Educational Maintenance Award (EMA)
An EMA is a means-tested award that provides eligible learners under 19 who are studying a full-time course at school or college with a cash sum of money every week. See page 98 for how you can access a website to find out more.

External verification
Formal checking of the programme by an Edexcel representative that focuses on sampling various assignments to check content, accurate assessment and grading.

Forbidden combinations
There are some qualifications that cannot be taken simultaneously because their content is too similar.

Functional skills
Practical skills in English, maths and ICT that enable people to work confidently, effectively and independently. Level 2 Functional Skills are mapped to the units of BTEC Level 3 National qualifications. They aren't compulsory to achieve on the course, but are of great use.

Grade boundaries
Pre-set points that determine whether you will achieve a pass, merit or distinction as the overall final grade(s) for your qualification.

Grading criteria
The specific evidence you have to demonstrate to obtain a particular grade in the unit.

Grading domains

The main areas of learning that support the learning outcomes. On a BTEC Level 3 National course these are: application of knowledge and understanding; development of practical and technical skills; personal development for occupational roles; application of PLTS and functional skills.

Grading grid

The table in each unit of your qualification specification that sets out what you have to show you can do.

Higher education (HE)

Post-secondary and post-further education, usually provided by universities and colleges.

Higher-level skills

These are skills such as evaluating or critically assessing information. They are more difficult than lower-level skills such as writing a description or making a list. You must be able to demonstrate higher-level skills to achieve a distinction.

Indicative reading

Recommended books and journals whose content is both suitable and relevant for the BTEC unit studied.

Induction

A short programme of events at the start of a course designed to give you essential information and introduce you to your fellow learners and tutors, so that you can settle down as quickly and easily as possible.

Internal verification

The quality checks carried out by nominated tutors at your school or college to ensure that all assignments are at the right level and cover appropriate learning outcomes and grading criteria, and that all assessors are marking work consistently and to the same standard.

Investors in People (IiP)

A national quality standard that sets a level of good practice for training and developing of people within a business. Participating organisations must demonstrate commitment to achieving the standard.

Learning outcomes

The knowledge and skills you must demonstrate to show that you have effectively learned a unit.

Learning support

Additional help that is available to all learners in a school or college who have learning difficulties or other special needs.

Levels of study

The depth, breadth and complexity of knowledge, understanding and skills required to achieve a qualification, which also determine its level. Level 2 equates to GCSE level and Level 3 equates to A-level. As you successfully achieve one level, you can then progress to the next. BTEC qualifications are offered at Entry Level, then Levels 1, 2, 3, 4 and 5.

Local Education Authority (LEA)

The local government body responsible for providing education for all learners of compulsory school age. The LEA is also responsible for managing the education budget for 16–19-year-old learners in its area.

Mandatory units

These are units that all learners must complete to gain a qualification, in this case a BTEC Level 3 National. Some BTEC qualifications have an over arching title, eg Construction, but within Construction you can choose different pathways. Your chosen pathway may have additional mandatory units specific to that pathway.

Mentor

A more experienced person who will guide you and counsel you if you have a problem or difficulty.

Mode of delivery

The way in which a qualification is offered to learners, for example part-time, full-time, as a short course or by distance learning.

National Occupational Standard (NOS)

Statements of the skills, knowledge and understanding you need to develop in order to be competent at a particular job.

National Vocational Qualification (NVQ)

Qualifications that concentrate on the practical skills and knowledge required to do a job competently. They are usually assessed in the workplace and range from Level 1 (the lowest) to Level 5 (the highest).

Nested qualifications

Qualifications that have 'common' units, so that learners can easily progress from one to another by adding on more units

Ofqual

The public body responsible for regulating qualifications, exams and tests in England.

Optional units

Units on your course from which you may be able to make a choice. They help you specialise your skills, knowledge and understanding, and may help progression into work or further education.

Pathway

All BTEC Level 3 National qualifications comprise a small number of mandatory units and a larger number of optional units. These units are grouped into different combinations to provide alternative pathways to achieving the qualification. These pathways are usually linked to different career preferences.

Peer review

This involves feedback on your performance by your peers (members of your team or class group.) You will also be given an opportunity to review their performance.

Plagiarism

The practice of copying someone else's work or work from any other sources (eg the internet), and passing it off as your own. This practice is strictly forbidden on all courses.

Personal, learning and thinking skills (PLTS)

The skills, personal qualities and behaviour that improve your ability to work independently. Developing these skills makes you more effective and confident at work. Opportunities for developing these skills are a feature of all BTEC Level 3 National courses. These skills aren't compulsory to achieve on the course, but are of great use to you.

Portfolio

A collection of work compiled by a learner, usually as evidence of learning, to present to an assessor.

Procrastinator

Someone who is forever putting off or delaying work, either because they are lazy or because they have poor organisational skills.

Professional body

An organisation that exists to promote or support a particular profession, for example the Royal Institute of British Architects (RIBA).

Professional development and training

This involves undertaking activities relevant to your job to increase and/or update your knowledge and skills.

Project

A project is a comprehensive piece of work, which normally involves original research and investigation by an individual or by a team. The findings and results may be presented in writing and summarised as a presentation.

Qualifications and Credit Framework (QCF)

The QCF is a framework for recognising skills and qualifications. It does this by awarding credit for qualifications and units so that they are easier to measure and compare. All BTEC Level 3 National qualifications are part of the QCF.

Qualifications and Curriculum Development Agency (QCDA)

The QCDA is responsible for maintaining and developing the national curriculum, delivering assessments, tests and examinations, and reforming qualifications.

Quality assurance

In education, this is the process of continually checking that a course of study is meeting the specific requirements set down by the awarding body.

Sector Skills Councils (SSCs)

The 25 employer-led, independent organisations responsible for improving workforce skills in the UK by identifying skill gaps and improving learning in the workplace. Each council covers a different type of industry.

Semester

Many universities and colleges divide their academic year into two halves or semesters, one from September to January and one from February to July.

Seminar

A learning event involving a group of learners and a tutor, which may be learner-led, and may follow research into a topic that has been introduced at an earlier stage.

Study buddy

A person in your group or class who takes notes for you and keeps you informed of important developments if you are absent. You do the same for them in return.

Time-constrained assignment

An assessment you must complete within a fixed time limit.

Tutorial

An individual or small group meeting with your tutor at which you can discuss your current work and other more general course issues. At an individual tutorial, your progress on the course will be discussed and you can raise any concerns or personal worries you may have.

The University and Colleges Admissions Service (UCAS)

UCAS (pronounced 'you-cass') is the central organisation that processes all applications for higher education (HE) courses.

UCAS points

The number of points allocated by UCAS for the qualifications you have obtained. Higher education institutions specify how many points you need to be accepted on the courses they offer. See page 98 for how you can access a website to find out more.

Unit abstract

The summary at the start of each BTEC unit that tells you what the unit is about.

Unit content

Details about the topics covered by the unit and the knowledge and skills you need to complete it.

Unit points

The number of points you gain when you complete a unit. These will depend on the grade you achieve (pass, merit or distinction).

Vocational qualification

Designed to develop knowledge and understanding relevant to a chosen area of work.

Work experience

Time you spend on an employer's premises when you learn about the enterprise, carry out work-based tasks, and develop skills and knowledge.

Please note that all information given within these useful terms was correct at the time of going to print.